THE WALLER JOURNALS

P D COTTON

Copyright © 2018 by P D Cotton.

ISBN   Softcover   978-1-948801-54-6

All rights reserved. No part of this book may be reproduced or transmitted in any form or by any means, electronic or mechanical, including photocopying, recording, or by any information storage and retrieval system without express written permission from the author, except in the case of brief quotations embodied in critical reviews and certain other non-commercial uses permitted by copyright law.

Printed in the United States of America.

BookWhip
1545 S. Harbor Blvd., #2001,
Fullerton, CA 92832

Dr. George & Sarah Waller
1880

To David G. Colley and all who served with the Twenty-Fourth
Virginia Field Hospital
past and present.

And to my wife Debbie, of over 47 years.
For her countless hours of proof reading my work,
and for putting up with me.

CONTENTS

Prologue ix
Chapter 1   Beginnings – Martinsville, Virginia 1
Chapter 2   Camp Pryor, Mid-1861 6
Chapter 3   First Manassas Junction, July 1861 8
Chapter 4   I Enlist, March 1862 13
Chapter 5   Second Manassas, August 1862 21
Chapter 6   Springfield Station, Fall 1862 23
Chapter 7   Sharpsburg, September 1862 26
Chapter 8   Fredericksburg, December 1862 30
Chapter 9   Late Winter 1863 34
Chapter 10   April 1863 36
Chapter 11   Taylorsville, May 1863 38
Chapter 12   Chambersburg to Gettysburg, July 1863 39
Chapter 13   Return to Virginia, 1863 45
Chapter 14   March 1864 47
Chapter 15   April 1864 49
Chapter 16   May and June 1864 51
Chapter 17   New Year 1865 58
Chapter 18   Retreat from Richmond to Sailor's Creek 61
Chapter 19   Return to Martinsville 65
Books/References 107
Acknowledgments 111
Final Notes 115

PROLOGUE

T his is not another Southern saga of the Great War of Secession that recalls only the glory of battle flags held aloft and the melody of bugles calling. This is the account of a Confederate Surgeon who, when just the right amount of moonlight and rye combined, would speak of those days to the youth who listened so eagerly, imagining it was himself performing noble deeds with unwavering courage.

Today, as I share his story, I too am a veteran of yet another great cause. I recognize in my own faltering pauses, those moments when he must have stopped short as he recalled another time and place, when, as a surgeon, bound by oath to snatch lives from the hands of the reaper and to give comfort to those about to cross over, all he could do was saw away at shattered bone and offer laudanum and whiskey. And I hear the cries of the countless fallen men blur into the sound of one man weeping for his brother.

CHAPTER ONE

Beginnings – Martinsville, Virginia

I was born on October 17, 1838, in Martinsville, Virginia, a pleasant little town just north of the North Carolina border, nestled in the foothills of the Blue Ridge Mountains. I was the fifth child of fourteen. Six died before the age of two. This left Mariah (Riah) Louisa, Sarah (Sallie), Mary Eliza, Samuel Gallatin, Judith Ann, William Duncan (called White because of his cotton blond hair), and the youngest, Lewis Skidmore, and myself.

Our plantation was established at Waller's Ford around 1760. We had a fine house built on a hill, with an enormous lawn sweeping down to the river. It was not the largest plantation in the area, but our fertile fields, tended by our sixty-one Negroes, produced high-quality tobacco, and we were quite well-off.

The entire Waller family was respected for their patriotism and public service. My great-grandfather, Col. George Waller, helped found Henry County, Virginia, and served as one of its first justices, as an early tax commissioner, as sheriff, and as one of Martinsville's first trustees. He was an officer in the local militia, which mustered on his plantation.

Colonel Waller fought at the Battle of Guilford Court House in 1781. His unit, mightily outmanned, was compelled to back down, but they gave Lt. Gen. Charles Earl Cornwallis a sound whipping even so. Afterward, Cornwallis remarked, "I never saw such fighting since God made me. The Americans fought like demons." Later, Colonel Waller had the satisfaction of being with General Washington when Cornwallis surrendered at Yorktown.

* * *

1859–1860, The Medical College of Virginia

I had the privilege of a fine education and, in the fall of 1859, went off to Richmond to attend the Medical College of Virginia. The tension between the North and the South was glowing red hot by then, and Gov. Henry Wise of Virginia encouraged Southern students enrolled in Northern schools to return to their home states. Our school gained two fine professors who returned from Philadelphia, along with many second-year students.

A hard-working student could graduate from medical college in about two years. The college held classes between November and March because cadavers did not do well in the summer months. The entire study consisted of six lectures: anatomy, chemistry, physiology, surgery, theory, and practice of medicine. A student must pass a written exam on one lecture before he could go on to the next. After graduating, students were required to do apprenticeship work under a practicing physician for two years or so.

The only pay professors received was from the sale of tickets to their lectures. We would buy lecture tickets from the professors at $15 each, so when two of the returning professors offered free tickets to their private lectures and quizzes, I eagerly took them all. Thanks to those extra studies, I was able to answer as well as any second-course student.

I was a serious young man and didn't allow myself to get as lathered up over the talk of the abolitionist plots and coming Northern invasion as so many others did. Perhaps I didn't take it seriously enough, but I viewed the news and trends of times with a cool eye. Besides, Richmond was a sophisticated city, and the gentry with whom I associated continued to attend balls, the theater, and discuss politics and commodities over aged whiskey and fine cigars.

My judicious calm proved profitable when I anticipated the drop in commodity prices as the Yankee bankers called in debts and hoarded money. I sold our family's bumper crop of tobacco early before the bottom fell out.

The recession deepened, and the gap continued to widen between Northern and Southern wealth. I was more afraid of the greedy New York financiers than of an unimaginable war until the presidency went to the know-nothing Republicans. Lincoln won the election, and the Southern states clamored for disunion.

We all continued to go through the motions of normal life even as South Carolina seceded, but by mid-February, eight more states seceded. Jefferson Davis was elected provisional president of the Confederate government. In an effort to avert bloodshed, the provisional Confederate congress sent a peace commission to Washington. Both President-elect Lincoln and Secretary of State Seward snubbed the delegates and refused them even the courtesy of a meeting. The insult was too much to ignore. War was inescapable.

* * *

April 1861, Virginia Secedes

On April 13th, the Union soldiers occupying Fort Sumter surrendered to the South Carolina Confederates. On April 17th, Virginia seceded. On April 18th, Robert E. Lee was offered command of the Union Army. After much soul-searching, Robert E. Lee resigned his commission with the Union Army and, on April 22nd, accepted command of the Virginia Forces. On April 28th, the Henry Guard formed in Henry County, Martinsville, Virginia.

My brother-in-law, Dr. Peter Reamey, was a brilliant man. He was able to read and write at the age of four and mastered Latin grammar by the age of five. He studied at Sullivan College in Columbus, Ohio, until in 1849. Then at twenty years of age, he married my sister Sallie. He graduated from the Medical College of Virginia just one year later in 1850.

It was only natural that Peter would be elected company commander of the Henry Guard. Peter's brothers, Henry Clay Reamey, John Starling Reamey, and Daniel Webster Reamey, along with my two grown brothers, Samuel G. Waller and William (White) Duncan Waller, signed on at once, eager to fight in Peter's company. On June 3rd, as Dr. Reamey led the Henry Guards out of Martinsville, the men were so certain they would crush the Northern invaders before the first frost that they packed as if leaving for a hunting trip. They whirled wives and sweethearts about gaily as they bade farewell. The women, as women will, wept and wrung their handkerchiefs. John Starling's wife held her hands over her still-trim belly, and stared after him with eyes moist and round, then scurried into the house retching.

The guards traveled by foot and then by train to Lynchburg to muster into service on June 5th, under Lt. Col. Daniel A. Langhorne. They were designated Company H of the Twenty-Fourth Virginia Volunteer Infantry.

As the first wave of young men marched off to rendezvous in Lynchburg, I returned to Richmond to continue my medical internship. Many of my fellows from Hampton-Sydney College decided to organize a company of their own. With the president of the school as captain, they officially mustered as Company G, Twentieth Virginia Regiment, "The Hampden-Sydney Boys." Again, I declined to join. It turned out to be a sensible decision on my part, for their career was a short one. In July, they were captured in the debacle that was Rich Mountain. In a generous and gentlemanly gesture, Gen. George B. McClellan paroled the young physicians-to-be on the condition that they return to their studies. They fled back to Richmond, much chastised, and not a little embarrassed.

CHAPTER TWO

Camp Pryor, Mid-1861

John Quincy Marr, captain of the Warrenton Rifles, became the first Confederate officer killed in action when a group of Yankee cavalrymen rode into Fairfax Courthouse on June 1st. They were on a scouting mission to learn the strength of our troops at Manassas Junction. They were repelled by Marr's well-trained men. Because the scouting party was thwarted in their attempt to spy on the strength of the Confederate forces in the area, the Union Army delayed a planned advance on Richmond.

Meanwhile, the Twenty-Fourth Virginia Volunteer Infantry, all men from the counties of Floyd, Franklin, Carroll, Pulaski, Giles, Mercer, (West Virginia), Patrick, Montgomery, and Henry, formed at Manassas Junction. The newly appointed major, Dr. James P. Hammed, was placed in charge of the troops.

After several days at the junction, the regiment marched to Davis Ford. They were rugged boys and, despite the hardships and intensity of the pace, arrived at their destination ready to guard the fords of the Bull and Occoquan Runs, just above where the two streams converged.

After reaching the Occoquan, they went into camp on the right side of the road, just behind a pine forest. Pickets were posted while the remaining troops settled into Camp Pryor, just three miles south of Manassas Junction.

CHAPTER THREE

FIRST MANASSAS JUNCTION, JULY 1861

Early in July of 1861, the Yankee army was heading south from Centerville as the Twenty-Fourth Regiment marched north to Manassas Junction to engage in what would become the first major battle of the war.

In an astonishing offense to humanity, the foolish Yankee women accompanied by their dandies drove out to the battlefield in carriages, carrying picnic baskets filled with delicacies and champagne. All atwitter, they waved their elegant plumed fans eager for an entertainment. Then the carnage began. The picnickers scrambled in horror to retreat. God would have at least a word to say about their debauchery. He opened the clouds of heaven, and loosed a deluge of rain upon their pretty parasols, streaked their powdered faces with mud, and mired their horses and carriages in clay rendered axle deep.

As the crowd of morbid sightseers struggled to flee, both armies clashed with a fury. Artillery and musket fire poured down on all within range. A cannonball hit several Union soldiers at once. Bodies and limbs flew. The ground exploded, and clumps of erupting earth darkened the sky as men screamed in agony and wild-eyed horses ran for their lives. The wise self-serving mules fled early in the outbreak, and were already far behind the battle lines.

Quickly, a temporary field hospital was established in a barn behind the Wilmer McLean house near the Orange and Alexandria Railroad. Before Manassas, my brother-in-law Peter Reamey wrote that he wished I were with him, but after, Peter changed his mind. In a letter to my sister Sallie, he described a new kind of horror. Maximum medical personnel for a regiment of over a thousand men were two surgeons, an assistant surgeon, and a hospital steward. The number of wounded brought in quickly overwhelmed the staff. A hole about the size of a cellar was dug in the yard by a detail of soldiers, and into this, the arms and legs were thrown as the surgeons amputated them. In the sweltering heat, the smell of ether and bloody mangled limbs was sickening, and the sound of men crying like boys was heartbreaking.

Following their victory at Manassas, the men of the Twenty-Fourth returned to Camp Pryor. My brother, White, wrote Mother from camp describing his experience in the battle. I would not have assaulted her with such strong language, as she is a fine and genteel lady, but gentlemanly manners seemed to elude White, who was young and brash. At any rate, White witnessed the battle and I did not. I include his letter here so you may read of it for yourselves.

After soundly rousting the Yankees at Manassas Junction, the Twenty-Fourth settled again into routine. They performed picket duty and marched, and countermarched between the Occoquan and Manassas Junction. The weather was hot and humid, and the bugs were a torment. The enlisted men dubbed Camp Pryor Camp Tick Grove. They groused about the monotony and nightly examined one another for ticks and lice. The Manassas plain was muddy and damp. Mosquitoes were abundant. Supplies were scarce, and tobacco, so prized, was utterly unavailable. By late July, the men were disease-ridden and miserable.

Two of Dr. Reamey's brothers had been sorely wounded during the battles at the junction. John Starling would have been left to die had not his brother Dr. Henry Clay discovered him as he, and the other hospital helpers searched for survivors who lay where they had fallen. As he struggled to retrieve his brother's poor broken body, a sniper felled him, not once but twice, and yet he persevered, and the two of them were loaded on a makeshift stretcher and carried back to the field hospital. Peter would not, could not, show preference to them, lest he lose the respect of the rest of the men, but allowed Henry Clay to continue treating poor John, long after he should have been relegated to the area for the hopelessly dying. On August 6th, John finally succumbed, and they buried him in a mass grave, along with the many others who had also bravely fought and slowly died there. Henry Clay, exhausted and ill, finally allowed himself to rest, but his wounds continued to fester, and inch by inch, the red streaks of blood poisoning crawled up his thigh until the end was inevitable.

Dr. Peter Reamey and Daniel Webster Reamey resigned, and together, they carried Henry Clay home to die with loved ones near. Daniel Webster took it upon himself to break the news of John Starling's death to his now visibly pregnant widow.

* * *

Finally, the last week of August, the Twenty-Fourth Regiment began to move. First, they made a new camp just north of Occoquan Run, a mile and a half in front of the mouth of Wolf Run. Then they moved to Fairfax Station to support Longstreet at Fairfax Courthouse. From there, they were marched to Mason's Hill, thirteen miles northeast of Fairfax Courthouse.

From Mason's Hill, the troops could look down on the United States Capitol building. The dome, although unfinished, was still under construction. President Lincoln felt that continuing the project despite the war was an important symbol to maintain public morale and faith in the United States. Over Georgetown Heights, a massive hot-air balloon sailed. A Union aeronautics professor, T. S. C. Lowe, kept a balloon in the air almost constantly. The young Confederates, most of whom had never before traveled more than a few miles from home, gazed upon these sites in wonderment.

While performing picket duties at Mason's Hill, they were drawn into intense skirmishing. After three harrowing days, they returned to Wolf Run and set up Camp Ellis. Good water and firewood were abundant, and so they remained, guarding the right flank of the Confederate Army.

Their relief was short-lived. Typhoid fever, pneumonia, and measles ran rampant. The Henry Guards were reduced at one point to only thirty men standing. At least one man died every day, and the men of that company claimed the regimental surgeon, Dr. Sterling Neblett, was indifferent to their suffering.

In late October, Governor Letcher presented each regiment from the Commonwealth with a Virginia State flag. He would then give a patriotic speech intending to boost the morale of the men. But the soldiers, drinking until drunk and discharging their weapons, preferred antic relief to the political niceties and successfully interrupted the ceremony.

Plans were made to remain in place for the winter, and the men of the Twenty-Fourth Virginia began building winter quarters, adding chimneys of clay and sticks to their tents, and hewing logs to build makeshift cabins. The gaps in the rough timbers were filled with mud, and clay and stick fireplaces were added. Rations were plentiful. Each man was issued a pound of flour or crackers, and half a pound of meat or fatback.

Though they were relatively comfortable, there was so little action boredom began to weigh on the men. Many took "French furloughs," unauthorized absences, but even so, few failed to return.

To everyone's great annoyance, the Confederate congress decreed that volunteers were to serve an extra year. Though the volunteers complained, they remained loyal to the cause and reenlistment continued.

CHAPTER FOUR

I ENLIST, MARCH 1862

As 1862 dawned, our hope for an early end to this war was gone. Battles were fought across the entire continent. Even in California, soldiers rose to arms. Instead of seeking a resolution to the dilemma of slavery and state's rights, the abolitionists laid a mantle of religious zeal upon the shoulders of their soldier boys. And the Yankees began to believe they were fighting for God, and holy redemption. One mother is said to have placed a shield in her son's hand as he enlisted, and instructed the captain that if her child could not return carrying it, he should be brought back to her laid upon it.

Various hospitals sprung up about the city, offering plenty of opportunity for us young doctors to practice and learn. No matter how diligently I labored, I gained no promotion from my studies, for the surgeons in charge continued to consider me as only a student. We interns were accused of callousness and cavalier ineptitude by the hospital directors. They then decided to recruit civilian women as nurses, citing their tender empathies as better medicine than what we could provide.

How could we have remained sane otherwise? The numbers of patients brought in were so great. Shadow-thin men came to us barely ambulatory, limbs shattered and missing, stinking from wounds riddled with flesh-eating disease or wasting from consumption. I learned early in my training that even the most skilled hands could not save a life too fragile to survive surgeries. So yes, perhaps my heart had grown hard but of a necessity, lest I become overwhelmed by the endless parade of suffering. No prayer could save a gangrenous limb. No strip of torn petticoat wetted with pious tears would cool the brow burning with erysipelas, called Saint Anthony's fire. To prevent the flames of disease from raging through the rest of the hospital, those poor souls who were infectious were simply placed in isolation to live or die as God chose. Those with incurable ailments were sent, whenever possible, to their homes to die in peace. I felt useless and despised as I struggled to save lives that could not be saved, and found that I could offer no comfort to the hopelessly dying.

The newspapers reported that a draft would soon be decreed to fill the gaping ranks on the battlefield. Only those who enlisted before conscription began would be allowed to choose the regiment or company to which they would be assigned. Anxious to be near my brothers and friends in Company H, I made my decision, and journeyed home to Martinsville to embrace my mother and sisters, perhaps for the last time.

Upon enlistment, I was given the rank of private and marched forth a simple foot soldier. I prayed that I would be assigned to serve in the medical field, not taking lives, but saving them as my physician's oath decreed.

Williamsburg, April 1862

We new recruits had barely found our bearings among the men of Company H when we were joined up with the Twenty-Fourth at Orange Courthouse, and Colonel Early marched us back to and through Richmond on April 8.

As we marched smartly down the main streets, the townsmen turned out to cheer us and wish us Godspeed. The ladies rushed up to us and pressed sweets and delicacies into our hands. We swelled with pride and gladly accepted these gifts, along with the tender kisses blown to us by the young girls waving from the windows and porticoes.

Then began the longest most arduous journey I thought I might ever have to take. We crowded aboard three sloops and a steamboat to Kings Mill Wharf. Without a break to rest, we were ordered to move south along the James River, and hurriedly marched toward Lebanon.

The rain was relentless. Downpours were relieved only by persistent drizzle. When we arrived at Lebanon, we slept on ground awash with rivulets of cold muddy runoff. The next morning we're up and off again for another twelve miles to Redoubts 4 and 5 at the extreme left of the Confederate lines. There, the soldiers secured the buildings, and burned an orchard, effectively destroying the hiding places from which the Yankees had been harassing our troops.

I was indeed assigned to the medical corps and found myself treating soldiers struck ill from the cold and fatigue. The exposure was as deadly as combat. Numbering only five hundred men, we were half a regiment. Two hundred lives were lost since they left camp at Manassas Junction three weeks earlier.

What was needed, we could not provide. Their tired bodies needed rest, warmth, and food. The rations were dismal. One fellow wrote home: "We have the worst water to drink you ever saw. We do not feast very high in the army. We draw pickled pork, flour and half rations of sugar and black eyes peas, but coffee we don't even get to smell."

Actually, the men had coffee, but the water from which it was made was barely fit to drink. They were allowed to draw only half rations. The flour was full of weevils and the sugar, ants. Most of the pickled pork was so unfit the men refused to eat it.

An infusion of recruits reached us at the end of April. For the most part, they were older than the boys who had originally enlisted and endured so much already. As predicted, the Conscription Act went into effect, and all white males between the ages of eighteen and thirty-five, and not legally exempted, suddenly found themselves members of the Confederate Army. The unwilling "volunteers" brought with them much grumbling and disaffection, and the troop's morale sank.

On May 3rd, we were roused and set out for Williamsburg. We were glad to be leaving; for we were mountaineers, and we feared we would be at a great disadvantage should we be engaged by gunboats from the water.

The rain continued to plague us. Mud and water sucked at our shoes, and the wagons mired to their axles. We marched through the night, and as the sun rose on Sunday, May 4th, we arrived at Williamsburg.

We rested briefly and fitfully, for as afternoon approached, we could hear musket fire. Soon we moved out on the double-quick, and again, as we marched through Williamsburg, the locals turned out, and their cheers emboldened us for what lay ahead.

Upon spotting the enemy, the scattered ranks were ordered to load and fix bayonets. The regiment advanced through the dense underbrush. When they reached the edge of the woods, they discovered the other units in the brigade were nowhere to be seen.

Receiving fire from both flanks and the front, men fell almost as fast and often as the rain. Nevertheless, the men continued to advance.

The regimental color bearer was in the front of the Twenty-Fourth, encouraging the men on, and as they moved closer to the enemies position, officers and men continued to fall. However, when they had advanced to within one hundred yards of the enemy, the panic-stricken Union forces frantically retreated. And the enemies fire slackened and finally ceased.

The regiment regrouped along a fence and prepared for the final charge. Then before they could advance, orders came down to turn back immediately.

From the first musketry, the litter bearers began bringing the wounded in from the field. The most devastating fire was the artillery. Bombs, balls, and grape shot were flying everywhere. At one point, as I leaned over a wounded man, picking shot from his body, a cannonball flew between my legs and struck the surgeon behind me. By instinct, I fell upon my patient to cover his body with mine. As I dropped my head, my life was saved, for at that moment, a musket shot skimmed across my skull, taking hair and scalp cleanly off. Though it bled profusely, I was, by God's grace, only briefly stunned.

Despite the shock of the grievous loss of one of our own fellows, I and the other medical staff remained at our makeshift operating tables all night and into the next day. Mutely, we went on caring for the wounded, arms and legs gone, gaping chest wounds. Some were carried in with their heads taken nearly off. We were beyond horror. We were completely numbed.

* * *

From September 28th to October 6th, the regiment performed picket duty at Springfield Station. While there, the men guarded the Confederate transportation lines.

Death became an everyday occurrence in Northern Virginia that summer. I could see the sick and dying at every turn and in my dreams. I could do so little to ease the suffering, and nothing to stop carnage. The best a doctor could do was keep doing his job.

As if dysentery and camp cough didn't add enough misery to the suffering of the soldiers, slackers also eroded the morale. They would whine and malinger, feigning illnesses in hopes of being relieved of duty. Slackers, who failed to perform their camp duties or refused to join the regiment when it went into battle, were a scourge.

Sensing that the army was going to remain stationed for the winter, we began constructing quarters. Happily, at Union Mills, rations were plentiful and camp duties were few. Now our rations consisted of a pound of flour or hardtack, and half a pound of meat, usually fatback. The soldiers' primary camp duties were quarters guard, more of an inconvenience than a hardship.

We got our news from one another, sharing snippets of gossip as we passed the time. Dr. Neblett's resignation was a topic one afternoon.

"Dr. Neblett left for home yesterday. I guess his resignation was accepted. He seemed to be very glad to get off."

"I, for one, am happy to see him go. Harrison is acting head surgeon of the regiment now."

Dr. Harrison called all the doctors together and addressed the group. "Gentlemen, I called y'all here to discuss the treatment of the patients we now have at hand until they can be transported to general hospitals. In winter camp, we shall be plagued with dysentery, typhoid fever, pneumonia, smallpox, and malaria."

Dr. Harrison turned to John Curd. John was from Goochland, Virginia, graduated from Jefferson Medical College, Philadelphia, 1855.

"John, procure all the fresh fruits and vegetables you can beg, borrow, or steal. We need them to treat scurvy. Also, check our quantities of whiskey and any dressings we have on hand."

Dr. Harrison was emphatic. "We want to be ready before the heavy winter sets in. Remember, diseases don't discriminate between enlisted and officers, so watch yourselves and keep fit."

Then he singled me out. "George, please check our quantities of blue mass. Can you tell us, George, tell me, what are blue pills?"

Relieved that I knew the answer, I replied, "Blue pills are a mercury-based medicine used in the field for constipation."

"Excellent. I shall entrust you to take care of our medical supplies. Check the quinine and morphine. See that the quartermaster orders whatever you and John think we shall need."

And so I received a promotion of sorts. Now I was hospital steward in charge of supplies. Perhaps I could finesse a bit of tobacco as well, for morale, of course.

* * *

Time passed, and the fighting went on. We participated in the battles of Seven Pines, Frayser's Farm, Malvern Hill, and the Seven Days Battle.

The Twenty-Fourth suffered heavy losses at the Battle of Frayser's Farm. At one break in the fighting, I ran into John Singleton, color bearer for Company B. He was sitting on a log, smoking a corncob pipe. I walked up to him. "John! How have you been?"

John looked up. "George, haven't seen you in a coons age. How is the doctoring business going?"

"It's a sorry business, that's what. How is the war going in your neck of the woods?"

"Well, the other day we was marching down at the creek at a double-quick—running, mind you—on one of the hottest days you ever saw, and all of a sudden, we come upon all this dead and wounded everywhere. Those of the wounded who could talk were telling us to hurry up and give them rascals a thrashing. One fella says, 'Boys, when you get there, just holler, and they'll run like varmints.'

"So when we reached the water's edge, where the Yankees were trying to cross, we give a helluva yell, and they all skedaddled just like he said they would, but they reformed and came at us to give it another go. But we was too much for 'em, and they scampered off into the brush. We never followed 'em 'cause we knew they'd be a layin' for us. Would have cut us all to pieces by means of hidden batteries. This was the fight on Thursday, you know, and on Sunday was big fighting . . ."

He tapered off, shaking his head. His shoulders sagged a bit.

"I know about Sunday's fighting." I didn't say more. We neither one wanted to bring that day back to mind.

CHAPTER FIVE

Second Manassas, August 1862

At 4:00 p.m., they advanced north in the direction of the Chinn house. The fighting began at 6:30 p.m. on August 28th.

The men were placed to the left of the brigade as they moved out in fine order. Traversing a cornfield, they continued toward the Chinn House. As they approached the house, their right came under fire at point-blank range from Union infantry hidden behind a stone wall. Suddenly, the entire brigade was engaged. Savage combat erupted between the Twenty-Fourth and an Ohio Regiment. After about ten minutes, the Union lines were flanked and turned back.

Continuing forward, the regiments became entangled as they passed the Chinn House. The commanding officers quickly reformed the regiments. It came right back into line. Advancing to within 250 yards of enemy batteries, they encountered severe canister shot. Still, they continued to close ranks around their regimental color bearer, Sgt. John Singleton.

The Virginians stormed into the enemy's works and fired a destructive volley into the enemy's ranks. Mounting the enemy's works, they overwhelmed the Union gunners who hastily retreated, leaving the Virginians in possession of their guns.

After the battle, our weary soldiers of the Twenty-Fourth proceeded to the rear. There, they received the first rations they had received in three weeks: rations of beef, coffee, sugar, and crackers.

The next morning we were up early. Once the company roll call was taken, the rain-soaked brigade headed across the battlefield, looking for lost comrades and burying the dead. The carnage of the previous day's battle covered the field with the dead and dying.

At a house converted into a field hospital, myself and the other doctors took no notice of the dawn. We were still busy at our tables. Saws and knives dripped with blood. The severed arms, legs, and fingers were discarded outside a window, forming a pile five feet high.

CHAPTER SIX

SPRINGFIELD STATION, FALL 1862

From September 28th to October 6th, the regiment performed picket duty at Springfield Station. Rations had been issued to the troops when they left Mechanicsville, but for the next two weeks, they had to live off the land. Green corn and unripe apples procured along the march constituted their basic diet. The Confederate Commissary Department could not keep up with the armies' rapid movements.

We were stalled at the foot of Thoroughfare Gap as the Union infantry blocked the narrow pass, thus detaining Longstreet's men. A flank attack by other Confederate units allowed Longstreet's forces to burst through the Gaps. Climbing over the dead bodies of the federals, the First Corps proceeded northward.

The lead brigade reached the north side of Bull Run Mountain, and we camped for the night. The next morning we finally reached

Manassas plain. The temperature was so hot the exhausted men drank from slime-covered ditches. At noon, the brigade halted three miles east of Gainesville. Then we were at once placed in a line of battle near Manassas Gap Railroad.

We remained there only a short time and then marched to a position east of the railroad. While the brigade proceeded east, the men were sent to support the artillery.

It was estimated that the Second Battle of Manassas cost the Union Army the following: 1,716 killed, 8,215 wounded, and 3,893 missing. And our brave Confederate soldiers suffered: 1,305 killed and 7,048 wounded or missing. The vast nameless and suffering wounded kept the other doctors and me working all that night and again into the next day.

On Monday, September 1st, after having won a stunning victory, our army began a new march. They passed over horrible roads and reached Chantilly. They remained a day near Chantilly foraging the countryside for food.

On the following day, September 3rd, they headed toward Leesburg. Passing through Frying Pan Church and Guildford Station, they exchanged greetings with the local citizens. Many of the ladies pushed gifts of food into the hands of the grateful young soldiers as they trudged along.

The column halted for the night just south of Leesburg. Up again, at 6:00 a.m. the next day, we passed through Leesburg, and by night of September 5th, we camped near Big Springs.

The next morning we crossed the Potomac River at White's Ford. There, at White's Ford, General Lee ordered all barefoot and sick troops to Winchester. Most of who went to Winchester were in real need of care. Some soldiers took advantage of the order and deliberately discarded their own shoes in order to avoid the Maryland campaign.

Predictably, our medical staff had to contend with chronic diarrhea that plagued the ranks because of their continual diet of green apples and raw corn. The weakened condition of the men, plus the extreme September heat, caused even more good men to straggle. Lice or gray backs, as they were called by the troops, added even more discomfort. Long forgotten were the young men's visions of dashing about riding fine steeds and wearing red sashes, brandishing their sabers as maidens swooned.

CHAPTER SEVEN

Sharpsburg, September 1862

On September 7th, the Twenty-Fourth headed toward Franklin. Arriving near there at 4:00 p.m., we remained two days as our troops destroyed the railroad bridge that spanned the river.

Maryland had mixed emotions about the Confederacy. On September 10th, when we entered Fredericksburg, the citizens there were only lukewarm toward the Southern cause.

The next day we took the Boonsboro Fredericksburg road to Hagerstown. There, we were treated like heroes. The people of Hagerstown provided food, clothing, and shelter. In return, men of the Twenty-Fourth protected a valuable supply depot in town.

On the morning of September 14th, we countermarched through the Hagerstown Road and headed for Boonsboro. As we marched down Hagerstown Road, we could hear Confederate forces engaged at Turner's Gap. Sensing the urgency of the situation, the soldiers stepped lively, advancing under orders even more quickly, despite the heat and dust.

Passing through one village, we saw our wounded comrades crowded on porches and lying in the streets. These Marylanders refused aid even to the wounded for fear of Union retaliation.

We passed through Boonsboro and proceeded on to Kingsville, where we camped for the night.

After breakfast the next day, we marched to the village of Sharpsburg. There, the army secured a position southwest of town. Over the ridge from their position was a brigade that spanned Antietam Creek. For the rest of the day, we rested while General Lee consolidated his army.

* * *

Bloody Lane, September 17, 1862

As the Twenty-Fourth awaited orders, less than a mile away, along the Sunken Road, a severe artillery duel occurred. The following morning of September 17th, cloudy skies shrouded the two armies facing each other on the fields of Maryland. The Confederates were ordered to dig in and defend. With the help of the artillery, they repulsed several Union advances. Late in the morning, the fighting advanced to the extreme right of the Confederate line. By 1:00 p.m., the Georgians were so outnumbered that they had to fall back from the hills overlooking the bridge. Driven from their stronghold, they rallied out of their exhaustion and, with great skill, withdrew, firing as they retreated.

Though outnumbered, the Confederates endured artillery fire and charge after charge for three and a half hours. The Southerners at last repulsed the federals. Five thousand, five hundred men from both sides were wounded or lost their lives on Sunken Road.

Blood flowed and mixed with the muddy mire of the road that ever after would be known as Bloody Lane.

* * *

In the meantime, the Twenty-Fourth had been detached from the brigade and reassigned to protect a Confederate artillery located along Harpers Ferry Road. This new position was approximately a mile from Burnside's Bridge which crossed Antietam Creek.

Burnside's onrushing federals pushed Jones's Confederate division into the outskirts of Sharpsburg. The Confederates bolstered their courage by repeatedly crying out to one another, "A. P. Hill is coming!" Their courage was rewarded. Gen. A. P. Hill's Light Divisions, who had marched his men seventeen miles in eight hours to arrive on the field from Harpers Ferry, eventually saved the crushed forces on the right and barreled into Burnside's exposed left flank. Everyone says the grueling march that brought General Hill's troops to the fray in the "nick of time" saved the Army of Northern Virginia.

That night the men received what rations that were available and slept uneasily on their arms. This was the bloodiest single day of the war so far. Could there be even worse yet to come?

* * *

On Thursday, September 18th, the two armies lay facing each other. The wounded continued arriving until the town was quite unable to hold all the disabled and suffering. They filled every building, and they overflowed into the country: farmhouses, barns, corn cribs. There were six churches, and they were full. Schoolhouses, the courthouse, the town hall, every inch of space, and yet the cry for more room could still be heard. In the unfinished town hall, they threw a few rough boards across the beams, placed piles of straw over them, placed a single plank to walk on, and declared it a hospital.

I told someone that yellow was the hospital color, and immediately, everybody with a yellow piece of cloth hung it over every house with wounded. The whole town was a hospital.

We waited all the next day for the federals to attack, but they did not. About nightfall, we received orders to prepare to move southward. All available Confederate medical personnel, along with all the civilian doctors in the surrounding areas, worked together on both Union and Confederate wounded until exhaustion caused their instruments to drop from their hands.

The people of Shepherds Town were very kind to our wounded. They loaded up as many of the wounded in every wagon they could find and headed toward Virginia.

The next morning, at seven o'clock, the troops reached the Potomac River. Under General Lee's watchful eyes, the Twenty-Fourth assisted the artillery and infantry as they crossed the river into Virginia.

We reached the valley turnpike and bivouacked by a large spring near Martinsburg, enjoying a much-needed rest.

The Yankee newspapers reported 12,410 Union wounded, killed, or missing. And the Confederates reported 10,700 Confederates wounded, killed, or missing. It was estimated later that the period from 6:00 a.m. to 6:00 p.m., the soldiers fell at a rate of about two thousand every hour, or thirty-five per minute.

CHAPTER EIGHT

FREDERICKSBURG, DECEMBER 1862

Word got out that General Burnside was now in command of the Army of the Potomac. He hoped to cross the Rappahannock River at Fredericksburg and then engage General Lee somewhere south of the historic old town. The Yankees camped at Deep Run, just southwest of Fredericksburg, for the remainder of the month as Burnside consolidated his forces along Stafford Height.

Once again, Lee countered the federal move and directed his army to proceed to Fredericksburg. On November 20th, our unit passed over rain and mud-filled roads in a long and slow march. We entrenched near Deep Run at the foot of a large ridge that ran parallel to the river. For the next two weeks, we were on either picket duty or searching for firewood.

Yesterday it commenced hailing, raining, and snowing until this morning; the sun was shining in all its brilliancy upon snow about one or two inches thick. The snow and cold caused so much discomfort, and the lack of shoes made the winter weather even worse. The men had to wrap their feet in rags or hay to prevent frostbite.

The army has had nothing to eat since yesterday morning, but we heard from some Yankee deserters that the Union troops were about as bad off as we were. Some of those who deserted said that they had almost nothing to eat and that many were barefoot and almost naked. They said soldiers would give an overcoat for a plug of tobacco anywhere and that thousands would desert if they could.

On December 11th, the men were but on alert because the federals were crossing the Rappahannock River. For the next two days, we continued to monitor the federals' action. On December 13th, they formed a line of battle.

In response, the brigade made its way through the fog-covered valley. My unit remained in a reserve position until 3:00 p.m. then moved to the Confederate left.

On the double-quick down the Telegraph Road, the brigade passed Lee's hill and turned to the left of the road. While on the march, they came under severe artillery fire, plus sporadic musket fire. They suffered several casualties. Then they advanced toward Marye's Height between Hanover Street and Plank Road. From this position, they witnessed several of General Burnside's assaults upon Marye's Height.

The Union Army's futile frontal attacks on December 13th against entrenched Confederate defenders on the heights behind the city, will be remembered as one of the most one-sided battles of the war, with Union casualties more than twice as heavy as those suffered by the Confederates.

The Confederate artillery on the heights and the infantry from behind a stone wall decimated the ranks of the onrushing federals. We could hear the prayers, cries, and curses of the wounded federals behind the wall throughout the night.

We had been experiencing brilliant displays of the aurora borealis soon after dark these nights. For half an hour, it showed very brilliantly, reaching to the mid-heavens in colors of yellow and red.

On the night of the second day of the battle, there was a singular appearance in the elements, the most singular that I ever saw in my life. Some said it was an aurora borealis or northern lights, but if it were, it was different from any I ever saw before. It rose on the side of the enemy and came up very near parallel with our line of battle and right over us. It turned as red as blood, but when it commenced rising, it looked more like the appearance of the moon rising than anything else I know to compare it to. The whole sky was a ruby glow, as if from an enormous conflagration, yet marked by the darting rays peculiar to the northern lights. It caused much surprise and aroused fears even of those far from superstitious. As the glorious colors illuminated the battlefield, they shone so brightly we could see the piles of dead and wounded. It was tortuous to see, and we grieved for them, but federal skirmishers made it too dangerous for us to help the wounded. All we could do was turn our eyes and ears away and try to rest up for the anticipated morning assault. As weary as we were, I do not believe many slept.

The following day, Sunday, December 14th, the army maintained their position at the stone wall. As the morning mist cleared, they quickly formed ranks and directed a withering fire into a nearby fence, which they mistook for an advancing line of federals. Later in the day, enemy sharpshooters opened a heavy fire in return.

At 10:00 p.m., another Confederate unit replaced my unit, so we marched back to Telegraph Road to our original camp at Deep Run.

At month's end, we were in winter camp, two miles north of Guiney Station, where the entire hospital was crowded with wounded and dying men. No space was left unoccupied. There were so many, and the wretched souls just kept coming in such great numbers. We tried but could not keep up.

CHAPTER NINE

LATE WINTER 1863

In mid-February 1863, we broke camp and headed for Richmond. After several days of miserable marching, we reached Hanover Junction and then proceeded to Manchester on the Richmond and Petersburg Turnpike. We remained there until March 1st and then marched to Prince George Court House. We stayed at Prince George Court House for three weeks.

While there, the brigade was ordered to witness a court-martial. Anderson (Andy) King, a member of our regiment, was convicted of cowardice at Sharpsburg. With the entire brigade watching, he was tied to a pole, his shirt removed, and thirty-nine lashes administered upon his bare back. He was dishonorably discharged and ordered from the regiment. This was a rare and awful scene for us. Until Sharpsburg, we had been relatively free of both deserters and cowards.

On March 21st, the regiment moved by rail to Goldsboro, North Carolina. To keep warm, we piled earth or sand into the center of the boxcars and built fires on the dirt. The fires produced a considerable amount of heat, but since there were no chimneys, we were covered with smoke and soot when we disembarked at Goldsboro. We camped on the outskirts of town.

The next day we boarded another train and headed for Kinston. Arriving there in the evening, we passed through the deserted village and established camp south of the Nesuse River. There, regimental drill and camp duties were reinstated.

CHAPTER TEN

April 1863

April 1st found us on picket duty along the Trent River. We anticipated heavy skirmish fire, but none occurred. Three days later, we returned to Kinston.

At 2:00 a.m. on April 5th, we crowed upon railroad cars and passed though Goldsboro and Weldon.

We went into regular camp at Franklin Station, where they drew rations of one-quarter pound of bacon and one and one-eighth pound of flour.

Most of the men were glad to be back in Virginia. We all agreed that North Carolina was the nearest place to nowhere we ever saw. All it had were low flat marshy dismal swamps.

The North Carolina expedition was unpleasant for the men, but it was useful for the Confederacy. The Southern troops went to North Carolina to protect the supply lines in the eastern part of the state. While the Virginians were in Eastern North Carolina, other Confederate units in the central part of the state collected valuable provisions for the Army of Northern Virginia.

On April 11th, with the rest of Longstreet's troops, the Virginians headed for Suffolk. Arriving there on April 13th, Kemper's men formed a line of battle and entrenched. The Twenty-Fourth Virginia spent three weeks on outpost duty southeast of the city. Skirmish fire erupted several times, but the regiment suffered no casualties.

At midnight on May 4th, the Twenty-Fourth Virginia left Suffolk and headed for Richmond. The men marched all night through swamps and water up to their waists. By midmorning of the next day, we passed through South Quay, where we rested for the remainder of the day. This thirty-two-mile march nearly devastated the men, yet on the morning of May 5th, the troops made ready to go again. After marching twelve miles, we camped for the night.

We finally reached Richmond on May 16th. Richmond was no longer the lively, happy town that I had known when I left medical school.

Just three days before we reached the capital, the body of Gen. Thomas J. (Stonewall) Jackson had been removed from the governor's mansion where it lay in state and sent to Lexington for burial.

They say he was killed by friendly fire in early May at the battle Chancellorsville. It is true he lost an arm from that unfortunate error, but it was pneumonia that killed him. Either way, the Army of Northern Virginia may not recover from the loss of this bold and valiant leader.

CHAPTER ELEVEN

Taylorsville, May 1863

We reached Taylorsville, a small village located just south of Hanover Junction. The men set up camp. Regimental drills were conducted twice a day. Rations of bread, bacon, sugar, and peas were plentiful. The time we spent in Taylorsville greatly improved the physical condition of the brigade. Rev. Theodorick Pryor put on numerous religious revivals throughout the spring and summer and into autumn. Chaplains held services in the evenings, and we were encouraged and uplifted by thousands of voices rising as they sang songs of praise unto God.

When orders came, as they must, we abandoned our Taylorsville camp and headed north. Three days of marching brought us to within ten miles of Culpeper Court House where we set up camp for three days' rest, then on to Berryville, where we were issued new uniforms.

As the Northern march commenced again, we passed through Darkesville, and Martinsburg, West Virginia… Hagerstown, Maryland… and Green Castle, and Chambersburg, Pennsylvania.

CHAPTER TWELVE

Chambersburg to Gettysburg, July 1863

We remained near Chambersburg guarding the Confederate supply lines. Upon our arrival, the local citizens greeted us with contempt, yet there were no acts of retribution against the Pennsylvania natives.

The regiment destroyed part of the Hagerstown and Chambersburg Railroad, as well as the depot and other buildings in the town. Company H acted as provost guards to ensure that the troops were not interrupted as they worked.

On this day, we rested from the previous day's labor.

At 2:00 a.m., we proceeded eastward on the Chambersburg Pike toward Gettysburg. Under a broiling hot sun, we rapidly crossed South Mountain and, by 2:00 p.m., had marched twenty-three miles through suffocating dust. Exhausted, we encamped near Willoughby Run. We were three miles from Gettysburg, which, for the previous two days, had been the scene of a desperate struggle.

As July 2nd came to an end, we had an uneasy feeling that tomorrow would bring us something we might not be ready for.

By 3:30 a.m., we broke camp and headed down the Cashtown Road for Gettysburg. Our brigade led the rest of Pickett's division and arrived just west of Gettysburg around 8:00 a.m. Under the watchful eye of Gen. Robert E. Lee, we headed south and began to discard all nonessential accoutrements. Along the march, we witnessed Confederate burial parties interring the dead of the previous day's battles. My uneasiness grew. This was not going to be a good day.

After a twenty-minute rest stop at Pitzer Run, we turned eastward. Around 11:00 a.m., the regiment, with the rest of the division, formed battle lines behind the crest of a ridge just west and south of the Spangler House.

An artillery battalion was stationed on the crest of Seminary Ridge to the front of us. Four hundred yards behind the artillerymen, the brigade aligned from left to right as follows: Third, Seventh, First, and Twenty-Fourth Virginia. The men remained in the open field behind the ridge for the next three hours sweating under a blistering sun. The men kept watch and waited.

I climbed to a high place just beyond the division field hospital at Breen's Mineral and Flour Mill. Using a pair of borrowed field glasses, I watched from the top of Seminary Ridge. At 1:00 p.m., our artillery commenced shelling the enemy position on Cemetery Ridge. The Yankee artillery quickly replied in kind, and the ground shook incessantly from the continuing artillery fire.

As I held the glasses to my eyes, I could see our men in the trees just behind the line of artillery. They were suffering considerably from shrapnel falling from the enemy's batteries. One of our officers suffered a painful head wound from the splinters of an apple tree struck by a Union shell. The merciless sun also battered the troops. Several men actually fainted from the heat. The brigade suffered more than a 50 percent casualty rate before the actual charge began.

At 1:45 p.m., General Longstreet gave the order for General Pickett to advance. I could see he had formed his division in two lines: Kemper's and Garnett's brigades in first, followed by Armistead's regiments. Once the consent to the charge was given, Pickett rode among his men.

At approximately 3:00 p.m., the Confederate artillery ceased firing and was given the order to move out. There was no cheering or the defiant rebel yell as in the past. Great determination was written grimly on the men's haggard faces as they prepared to take the enemy position.

The men moved quickly and then headed eastward. My company, Company H, acted as skirmishers two hundred yards in advance of the main assault line. From my vantage point on Seminary Ridge, I could see them cross a double fence at Spangler's lane and then reform their lines. The brigade had never looked better. I felt a great pride for their courage and sorrow too for the many that would soon fall.

Upon crossing the plain below, the Twenty-Fourth moved repeatedly to the right and then by the left flank in a northeasterly direction to avoid drawing enemy fire.

Once the division had cleared the ravine and neared the Emmetsburg Road, they received a devastating fire by Yankee artillery batteries located on Little Round Top. Their exposed flank made an inviting target, and the enemy artillery hit with increasing frequency.

The artillery fire was just getting going when the Twenty-Fourth came under concentrated musket fire by enemy infantry.

Continuing eastward, Kemper's brigade passed the side of the Codori house. After the brigade cleared the house, they met with more Union infantry in force. A Vermont brigade, located in a cluster of trees southeast of the Codori house and perpendicular to the Yankee line, took further advantage of the Virginians' exposed right flank.

Musketry ripped huge gaps in the ranks of the regiment, but the Twenty-Fourth pushed forward, only to be hit from the front by more Yankee infantry.

Despite the devastating fire from enemy infantry, the men from the Virginia highlands continued to close ranks and follow their color bearer, Charles P. Belcher.

Through the smoke of the artillery fire, I could identify each regiment and their position on the field by their color bearers. Each bore a distinct flag designed for his unit, and were a bearer to fall, another would immediately take the flag and raise it again, rallying the courage of his brothers in arms.

This battle brought forth my memories of the battle in Fredericksburg, except this time it was the enemy who had the high ground. I thought it was more than I could bear. My heart constricted and my stomach turned over and spilled out its contents.

The regiment now opened fire pouring well-aimed volleys into the ranks of their Northern adversaries. In the confusion of battle, Kemper's brigade had drifted to the left. I raised my glasses again and watched as savage hand-to-hand combat began just south of the angle.

Despite the Yankees advantage of the stone wall, at least part of the Twenty-Fourth was able to open a breach. As the Confederates stormed over the wall, I saw some of the Yankees surrender. Continuing forward, Company E was able to occupy at least one of Union guns, but unsupported, they could not maintain their advantage. A Union counterattack swept the men back across the stone wall, and the troops were forced to retire.

As I looked to my right, I saw General Kemper paddle by on a stretcher. Disheartened, I could watch no longer.

As I made my way back to the hospital, stretcher bearers were already making their way off the field and heading for the hospital. When I walked into the hospital, the other surgeons were already at their positions. I just stood there staring around the hospital. The other surgeons were standing by their tables covered with blood. One was amputating a young patient's leg; I judged the suffering boy to be no more than nineteen. Another surgeon had his hand deep inside the abdomen of another man.

Then I thought to myself, *My god, what are we really doing here? Are we helping these men, or are we just prolonging their pain and suffering?*

I took my place at my improvised operating table, I tried to close off my mind from the horror and face my own duties. A young man lay screaming in front of me, his right arm severed just below the elbow. I quickly applied a tourniquet so I could more closely examine his wounds. With the flow squelched, I looked into his contorted face. He was not much older than sixteen. For a brief moment, I lost control. "Why are all of these just boys?"

I would have begun sobbing but for the stretcher bearer who had brought him in. He laid his hand on my shoulder and said, "If you don't help him right now, Doctor, he will die a boy."

It was the encouragement I needed. After the young man received chloroform, I completed the amputation the Yankee bullet had already begun, dressed the stump and turned him over to an assistant for his post-op care.

All night and into the next day, I labored at my table. At last, I found a moment to break away, so I went out the back door of the mill to get a bit of fresh air. As I walked around the house, dawn was just breaking. For a moment, I drank in the beauty of the spreading light turning the dark sky to cerulean blue, and then I turned a corner and ran into a pile of body parts the assistants had discarded out a window. So numbed was I, I felt no despair, only disgust. I went back into the hospital and resumed my duties at my table.

CHAPTER THIRTEEN

Return to Virginia, 1863

By early afternoon, it became apparent the Yankees were not going to counterattack, so orders were issued to the battered army to prepare to return to Virginia. The line of wagons loaded with the sick and wounded stretched along the road for eighteen miles. The dead lay where they had fallen alongside the dead or dying horses and mules. Flies swarmed. The bitter incense of death wafted skyward. Men cried out to God. Jesus wept.

On the march back to Virginia, we, along with the remains of Pickett's division, were detailed as provost guard. The men who drew this duty were charged with the distasteful task of taking four thousand Yankee prisoners back to Virginia. Torrential rains added to the misery but mercifully hid the tears that fell unbidden from empty eyes sunken in faces slack with horror.

By the evening, we reached Monterey on top of South Mountain. The First, Third, and Twenty-Fourth Virginia crossed the Potomac and began picket duty a mile south of the ferry. For the next two days, we guarded the roads while Lee's army crossed back into Virginia.

During the early fall of 1863, Kemper's brigade began to recover somewhat from Pickett's Charge. At Taylorsville, the troops had built substantial quarters. The men were issued new uniforms and brogans. I oversaw the replenishment of the medical supplies. Still, rations were minimal and the men remained thin and undernourished.

As we went into winter, we were more apprehensive than we were last year at this time. The ultimate victory, which we had hoped for in 1863, had not materialized. Instead, defeat had fallen on the Army of Northern Virginia.

General Pickett's division was cut to pieces at Gettysburg, suffering over 50 percent casualties. What the coming year would bring to the survivors, we could not know. However, we were by no means ready to quit, for though it was horrendous, we told ourselves it was, after all, only one defeat. Perhaps the coming new year, 1864, was the year we would claim victory.

CHAPTER FOURTEEN

March 1864

By March 5, 1864, we arrived by train at Wilmington. The following day we embarked on the English steamer, *Cape Fear*, which transported us to Smithville at the mouth of the Cape Fear River. We went into camp a mile south of the town.

By March 14th, we had established camp inside the confines of Fort Caswell, just across the bay from Smithville. The exact reason for this move is unknown.

While at Fort Caswell, the men of my unit were assigned to man the fort's heavy artillery. In order for the men to learn their artillery assignments, company officers drilled them twice daily. These drills were in addition to guard duty and infantry drills.

One night in the middle of March, a Confederate blockade runner ran aground near Fort Caswell. The men quickly took possession of the steamer and manned the ship's gun, thereby preventing a federal patrol from capturing the vessel. The mountaineers accomplished this mission without incurring any casualties.

For the highlanders, the North Carolina coast had proved a grand experience. Walking along shell-covered beaches, watching sea animals, and gathering oysters intrigued the men. A steady diet of fish and oysters was a great relief from fatback and beans. The men quickly learned to prepare oysters by cooking them in the shell, eating them raw or baking them in corn dough.

On March 23rd, the regiment prepared to leave their seaside resort, and on March 24th, the troops again boarded the steamer *Cape Fear* and headed to Wilmington.

The fruit trees had been in full bloom on the lower Cape Fear River. Much to their disappointment, the men found two inches of snow on the ground when they disembarked at Wilmington. From there, we took cars to Goldsboro.

CHAPTER FIFTEEN

April 1864

We remained at our old camp until April. We moved out, and by April 3rd, the troops had trudged through snow and mud to Tarboro. There, they camped on the east side of the Tar River. In this camp, we became part of Gen. Robert F. Hoke's command.

As of April 15th, Hoke's forces consisted of Terry's, Ramsom's, and Hoke's brigades, plus the Thirty-Eighth Virginia Artillery Battalion. Terry's men headed for Plymouth, an important Union supply depot, and arrived two and a half days later.

That evening, on April 17th, the Twenty-Fourth Virginia and her sister regiments advanced as skirmishers. We met some Yankee pickets at War Neck and drove them back into the Union lines at Fort Gray. For the next two days, we occupied several different positions along the Confederate lines.

On April 19th, we joined Hoke and Ransom in an assault on the east side of Plymouth. However, the attack failed.

On April 20th, Major Hambrick commanded the Twenty-Fourth in its assault on Plymouth. Once again, Lieutenant Colonel Maury was absent from the regiment; Captain Bentley asserted that Maury was absent without leave and retained his commission only because of "influence at court." Although ill himself, Captain Bentley performed the duties of the major.

The exact movements of the regiment during the battle are unknown to me. However, in all probability, the regiment was somewhere to the rear of their initial assault by Hoke and Ransom. In any case, the causalities were exceedingly light. It is likely that the regiment helped secure the town once Hoke's forces had affected the surrender of Gen. W. H. Wessell.

The extremely low casualty rate suffered by the regiment supports the assumption that the regiment was not actively involved in the assault. Only two men were killed and six wounded.

CHAPTER SIXTEEN

MAY AND JUNE 1864

The capture of Plymouth netted the Confederacy 1,600 prisoners and 2,000 small arms. Terry's men collected food, boots, and other personal items. However, by April 26th, the brigade had abandoned the plunder of Plymouth and marched to Washington via Jamesville.

At Washington, Terry's men formed battle lines, but the enemy had already evacuated the town.

On April 29th, the troops proceeded as far as Greenville.

There, we remained until May 2nd, when Terry's brigade headed for New Bern. The brigade arrived there on May 5th and formed lines of battle on Colonel Hill's farm. We expected to attack at any time, but once again, we were ordered to fall back to Kinston.

On May 8th, we reached Kinston and, the following day, took a train for Virginia. We rode the train into Jarrett's Station, Virginia, on the morning of May 10th. We had to disembark and march eleven miles to Stony Creek. There, we secured another train and headed for Petersburg.

This detour was necessary because General Kautz's Yankee cavalry had destroyed the railroad bridge just north of Jarrett's Station.

Upon our arrival at Petersburg, we received a hearty welcome from local citizens who feared Benjamin Butler's forces north and east of the city.

Our whole brigade camped for the night east of the Richmond-Petersburg Turnpike along Swift Creek. There, the troops laid on their arms in anticipation of a Yankee assault.

On the following day, May 11th, the enemy withdrew and the Virginians proceeded to Port Walthall Junction.

While there, the men spotted a large Union force and prepared to drive them away. However, the federals were in no mood for a fight and quickly retreated.

On May 12th, Terry's brigade took the Richmond-Petersburg Turnpike to Halfway House. During the march, the Confederate rear guard was harassed by Union skirmishers but no engagement occurred.

That evening the rain-soaked men once again formed battle lines, with the same results as before.

After the enemy retired, the regiment marched to the outer line of the works near Richmond-Petersburg Railroad. Later that night, they proceeded to a line of breastworks at Broad Rock racecourse near Manchester.

For two days, they impatiently remained behind the earthworks.

Finally, May 14th, they started for Drewry's Bluff. There, they secured a line of breastworks near Rice's Station between the

Richmond-Petersburg Railroad and the Richmond-Petersburg Turnpike.

At 7:00 p.m. the following day, they moved eastward, closer to Drewry's Bluff. There, they halted in a small forest on the left of the Stage Road. While in the forest, sixty rounds of ammunition were distributed to the men. Every man in the regiment knew that this meant there was to be a fight.

At dawn on May 16th, the brigade silently moved north on the Stage Road. They crossed Kingsland's Creek and formed a line of battle in a mist-shrouded valley.

Once again, they were on the right flank of the brigade. Across an open field and behind breastworks was the enemy. Quietly yet impatiently, they waited.

About 7:00 a.m., the lines formed. General Archibald Gracie's Alabama brigade, which was in front of the Twenty-Fourth, suddenly advanced. Then the Twenty-Fourth slowly followed. Skirmish fire quickly erupted, and without hesitating, Gracie's brigade lunged forward. Even with desperate fighting, Gracie could not take the enemy line. Moments later, an officer from the Alabamian's staff galloped up to the Twenty-Fourth and shouted, "Hurry up, boys! They are tearing us all to pieces." As Gracie's men were retreating through the lines, Colonel Terry ordered the regiment, along with the Eleventh Virginia, to move forward. Under Lieutenant Colonel Maury, they raced to the rescue of the Alabamians. Without a single man holding back or falling from the ranks, they stormed the Union position while the other regiments of Colonel Terry's brigade conducted a flank attack on the Union position. In less than fifteen minutes of fighting, the regiment lost more than one half of its members. Savage hand-to-hand combat ensued as the regiment grouped in the fog and smoke trying to find the heart of the Union resistance. After about an hour of fighting, they had given Charles Heckmen's federal brigade a sever beating. The entire Union line was theirs.

Once again, the Twenty-Fourth had suffered the highest casualty rate in the brigade: 28 killed and 108 wounded. All of Company F were either killed or wounded. Major Hambrick was mortally wounded, and Lieutenant Colonel Maury was also wounded. As always, the Twenty-Fourth paid an extremely high price for their success.

When the battle ended, they collected prisoners and any booty that the federals left behind. The men constructed some addition earthworks and advanced a skirmish line in case Butler tried to retake the fort. For the next three days, picket duty occupied the time of Terry's brigade.

After beating up Butler south of the James River, General Lee ordered Terry's men to head for Spotsylvania, where the Army of Northern Virginia was in a desperate struggle with Grant's Union forces.

On May 19th, Terry's brigade paraded through the streets of Richmond with a Union flag captured at Drewry's Bluff. That evening, part of Terry's brigade headed for Milford Station. However, the men from the Virginia highlands remained in Richmond until the following day, at which time they headed for Hanover Junction.

The Twenty-Fourth Virginia arrived at Hanover Junction on May 22nd, and there rejoined their units of the brigade.

On the night of May 23rd, the men marched to Andersonville, where, on the following day, they constructed a line of breastworks. The troops spent three days at Andersonville and then marched seventeen miles through a blinding rain to Atlee's Station. On

May 28th, the brigade proceeded to advance three miles north of Mechanicsville. Two days later, they camped near Cold Harbor.

Terry's brigade constantly changed position in order to stay ahead of Grant, as the Union General slowly encircled Richmond.

For the next two weeks, the brigade remained behind breastworks and braved Union skirmishers. While the Virginians were trapped in their trenches, other Confederate units were heavily engaged at Cold Harbor. On June 3rd, Grant's impetuous charge on the Confederate line was bloodily repulsed. However, the Union forces did not charge the part of the line occupied by the Twenty-Fourth Virginia. At 8:00 a.m. on June 13th, Terry's men changed positions. Heading south, the troops marched over the old battleground at Gaines's Mill, and camped for the night near Frayser's Farm. By June 16th, the men had marched up Darbytown Road, crossed the James River at Chaffin's Bluff, passed Fort Darling at Drewry's Bluff, and had taken the Richmond-Petersburg Turnpike to a position just north of Port Walthall Junction.

While marching down the Richmond-Petersburg Turnpike, the Virginians received gunfire from the enemy who held the road. Pickett's division quickly formed a line of battle and drove back the Union forces. Darkness quickly prevailed and prevented the Virginians from completing their task. However the men did retake the Confederate first line of works. During this engagement, Lieutenant Colonel Maury was shot through the hips. His wounds were so severe that he was never able to return to the field. Major Bentley was promoted and took command of the regiment.

The following day, June 17th, opened with heavy skirmishing. Later that evening, the regiment launched an assault along the entire Union line.

Charging near the Clay House, Pickett's division was able to recapture the Confederate outer lines of communication between Richmond and Petersburg. Despite the heavy infantry fire, the unit only suffered minor casualties.

The work performed by the Twenty-Fourth Virginia at the Clay House did not go unnoticed. General Lee was so pleased at the division's performance that he issued a special order congratulating them for their efforts.

On June 19th, they moved to a position near Swift Creek, remaining there only until that evening. The brigade countermarched back to their camp near the Clay House. There, they constructed fortifications and performed picket duty. The monotony of standing guard duty was broken for the men by daily skirmish fire between the unit and their Northern adversaries.

For the rest of June and half of July, they remained behind the breastworks. These works, known as the Bermuda Hundred line, ran from the James to Appomattox River north and east of Petersburg, and west of Port Wiltham Junction. The fortifications provided adequate protection from the enemy as long as the Confederates didn't venture beyond them.

Around the middle of July, they secured a position on a high piece of ground behind a skirt of timber midway between the Hoelett House and Swift Creek. There, the men constructed addition breastworks. While near Petersburg, they had a good view of the Union shells as they daily bombarded the city. Private Worrell believed that the shells had little or no effect on the city.

The regiment quickly made friends with the Union pickets, trading tobacco for bacon, coffee, sugar, and soap. In this way, they secured at least adequate rations. From time to time, the men would supplement their diet by raiding the Union supply of beef.

Remaining on the Howiett Line for the rest of the year, they had good winter quarters, which consisted of log cabins. However, drilling, guard, and picket duty kept the men from getting too comfortable in their quarters.

During the winter of 1864–1865, I was promoted and left in charge of the field hospital.

Picket duty was an arduous task for the troops. Walking their post every third night, they were greatly exposed to the elements. Consequently, they incurred a considerable amount of sickness; chills and fever were a constant trial for me.

Such privation caused one solder to write that the men were determined not to stay in the army longer than spring.

CHAPTER SEVENTEEN

New Year 1865

New Year's Day 1865, our regiment was in camp near Chester Station. The ladies of the Richmond-Petersburg area provided the New Year's Day dinner. They served turkey, beef mutton and apple butter, and apple pie. We were luckier than most other regiments in the food we received.

On January 3rd, we woke to an inch and a half of snow in the trenches of Petersburg. This snow offered the men an excellent opportunity to chase the "old Hare."

Rabbit chasing was one of the few camp diversions, which had only positive benefits for the men. I heard Private Penn reported seeing as many as fifteen soldiers after a single rabbit.

For the first two months of the new year, the men continued the monotonous work of drill, picket, and breastwork construction.

Desertion, by now, was epidemic in Pickett's division, as well as in the Twenty-Fourth Virginia. Men began to desert in groups of five, ten, or more. Hunger, lack of confidence in the success of the Confederacy, late pay, plus letters from home underscoring the numerous privations, which wives and family endured, caused the men to leave the ranks in ever-increasing numbers.

On February 26th, I became very ill with chill and fever. Later, I developed pneumonia, and I was sent to the Chimborazo Hospital No. 3 in Richmond. While there, I regained my strength with a good diet, but because I had abscesses in my lungs, I was compelled to remain in the hospital until the end of the war. I will recount the reports as they came to me.

On March 5th, the brigade was once again on the move. I heard reports that my division was headed for Richmond, but the march was halted by torrential rain bogging them down within two miles of Chester Station. They spent their days waiting for the roads to dry.

On March 9th, they reached Manchester. The following day the troops passed through Richmond and halted in the Confederate trenches near Brook Road.

Early on March 11th, they moved along the line of works to a position on Nine Mile Road.

The following day the Twenty-Fourth Virginia countermarched back to the trenches along Brook Road.

During March 14th through March 23rd of 1865, the men sought to foil General Philip Sheridan's federal cavalry raids on Richmond. Sending infantry to chase mounted cavalry was ludicrous, but the Confederate cavalry was so reduced that no other alternative was available.

The Virginians reached Richmond on March 25th and took the train to Dunlap's Station. On March 29th, the men crossed the Appomattox River five miles above Petersburg.

Once across the river, the troops took the Southside Railroad to Sutherland Station. By sending Pickett's division to the extreme right of the Confederate works, Lee continued to stretch his already thin lines.

CHAPTER EIGHTEEN

Retreat from Richmond to Sailor's Creek

On March 30th, they left Sutherland Station and headed southwestward. The rain-soaked Virginians were once again trying to stay one step ahead of Grant's men. On approaching Hatcher's Run, a Confederate cavalry picket reported that federals held the fort.

The Twenty-Fourth Virginia was immediately ordered to lead the march and storm the crossing. Mustering the same spirit that led us across the open plain at Williamsburg and up Cemetery Ridge, the men went to work. The men poured a devastating fire into the federal ranks and quickly routed the Yankees. Evening found them at the road junction known as Five Forks. It was from this point that the ever-offense-minded Lee planned to deliver another attack on Grant's advancing line.

Concerning the troops of Pickett, William H. Wallace, Matt Ransom, and Fitzhugh Lee's cavalry, General R. E. Lee ordered the Confederate forces to cross Chamberlain's Creek and drive the enemy southward.

The following morning, March 31st, they headed for Dinwiddie Court House. The brigade once again engaged in a lively skirmish, this time at Chamberlain's Creek. The Third Virginia led the way and forced the federals to a position south of the creek. With the rest of Terry's brigade following, the Virginians steadily pushed the enemy southward.

By nightfall, they had advanced to within a mile of Dinwiddie Court House. There, the whole regiment remained until 2:00 a.m., at which time Pickett's unsupported division headed back to Five Forks.

General Terry was injured when his slain horse fell upon the general's leg. Because of this, Col. Joseph Mayo temporarily took command of the brigade. Reaching Five Forks at dawn, the weary troops began erecting breastworks to prevent the Yankees from seizing the Southside Railroad.

Pickett posted his men facing southward along an east-west thoroughfare known as White Oak Road. The remnants of the brigade secured a position to the right of the fork. Stuart's men were on Terry's left. Corse's brigade was to the right.

By noon, the Virginians had felled trees and dug trenches. Finally, the exhausted men, many of whom had been without sleep for forty hours, completed their defense line.

Suddenly, to the east, the sound of battle became clearly heard to the regiment. Then without warning, the skirmishers were engaged and overran. The Union forces comprised of dismounted cavalry and infantry rushed headlong into the Confederate works.

After repulsing the several federals assaults, they were forced to change fronts when a part of General Gouveneur Warren's Corps broke through the Confederate line east of the Twenty-Fourth position. In order to meet this challenge, General Terry's brigade moved to the left of and perpendicular to White Oak Road. They managed to hold their positions but were overwhelmed by numerically superior Union forces. They were almost completely captured. Only a few of the men were able to escape the swarm of blue coats who took the Confederate line.

During the night of the battle, on April 1st, General Pickett's fragmented division regrouped along the south side of the railroad. Early the next day, the worn troops headed westward along the Appomattox River. The men reached Amelia Courthouse at dusk. There, they rested briefly before resuming the march for Farmville. Three days later, they joined the rest of General Lee's retreating forces, and by April 5th, the hunger-ravished men had established camp near Sailor's Creek.

The following day General Pickett's beleaguered division fought a rear guard engagement in order to allow the rest of General Lee's forces to escape. Outnumbered and physically exhausted, they were barely able to hold out until nightfall, at which time most of the remaining men of the Twenty-Fourth were either surrendered or captured.

* * *

Appomattox Court House

The Twenty-Fourth Virginia, once more than one thousand strong, now numbered only twenty-three men. Along with the other Confederates, the men of the Twenty-Fourth stacked their weapons at the courthouse and wept as their battle flag was handed over in surrender. The Twenty-Fourth Virginia disbanded at Farmville.

EPILOGUE

RETURN TO MARTINSVILLE

After being released from the hospital, George took the fragmented train line from Richmond back to his beloved home of Martinsville to rebuild his war-torn town. In 1868, George married a lovely girl from North Carolina, Sarah Louise Putzel. They went on to have seven children: George, Mary, Edmund, Crawford, Janie, Samuel, and William.

His wife, Sarah, was instrumental in building a monument to the Confederate Dead in Martinsville.

Besides being a practitioner of medicine and health officer, he also filled other prominent positions. He was elected councilman, magistrate, and mayor of the town of Martinsville. In every position, he measured up to the highest standards.

All his life, George practiced medicine in Martinsville, where he died on February 2, 1915, at the age of seventy-six.

George's wife Sarah Putzel Waller, died in 1921, surviving her husband George by six years. It is said that during Stoneman's raid through Henry Country, Sarah appealed to the federal officers and protected her invalid mother by her captivating manners and in return for this kindness gave them breakfast.

George lost two brothers in the war: William Duncan Waller (White), killed in battle on January 28, 1865, and Samuel Gallatin Waller, died on April 5, 1864.

George's sister Sallie, who went on to marry George's friend Peter R Reamey, died May 15, 1866. After Sallie's death, Peter R. Reamey re-married Elizabeth "Betty" Willis.

Peter R. Reamey died in June of 1891.

Letters – January 8, 1860, through October 23, 1864

Richmond Va
Jan 8th 1860
The widow Dandridge's

Dear Riah,

As this isn't a leisure day and I have nothing to do for it is too wet to go to church I will write you a few lines. I have not heard a word from home since I left so you will please write as soon as possible and let me know how grandma is and how Dink's cold if she has gotten over it. Tell grandma when you see her that I made the arrangement about her butter and she can send it when she pleases.

They said in Danville that they would be glad to get it. The City has been very slick ever since I have been here but it is melting off today

I have just returned from college. Mr. London of this city gave us that is the students a long lecture on moral philosophy which was a very able thing but it was not his production it was of Alexander Campbell - he London will lecture every Sunday morning at 9 o:clock on some passage of scripture in the college. The Sycamore church has given us an especial invitation to their church - The young men's Christian association has also given us an invitation to their hall at any time and to call on them at their rooms and also to use their library which is a very large and well assorted one in fact the whole city seems to feel a deep interest in the medical school. Our rooms are quite full everyday now and they have not all come in yet from their Christmas holidays, they are coming in every day

Tell White that there are a good many of his acquaintances here from the University and one of his special friends (Sykes) and probably a great many more.

I have not formed the acquaintance of them yet; the students all seem to be very well pleased with our professors, old Tucker especially. They have been recapitulating for their students benefit. Tell the Doctor when you see him that I am doing better now than I have since I have been here That two professors Tucker and Maguire came on from Philadelphia with the students They have their private lectures and quizzes and when they came here they gave to our students free tickets for which we are under many obligations to them for I believe that they are more improving than the regular lectures. They are both very good lecturers too. They quiz us on the regular lectures and they quiz closely too. Harry and I took them all and I reckon that you will think that I brag, but I believe that we answer as well as any of the second course students. I think that our students ought to make them both a nice present at the end of this session. They lecture on all of the branches and practice surgical anatomy and then quiz on all the branches also.

I went to the theatre last night for the first time since I got back and saw three pieces played (Asholians old guards, The spirit of the Rhine and I have forgotten the other it was something about Washington)

The old guards and the spirit of the Rhine were very good there are two famous players on the stage now Mr. and Miss Richings. The lady is one of the prettiest women I ever saw Harry says that she is the best looking he ever saw she is a very accomplished songstress (sings splendidly) she acts very finely also.

When you write (which must be as soon as convenient) let me know how the fuss came out about the dance that was at Laurel

Ridge. I have heard since I have been here that it was raging furiously but I reckon that there certainly will be calm after the storm has past, if the laws of nature hold good.

Give all enquiring friends my highest regards
And I am at the same time
as ever very truly yours affect brother
Geo. E. Waller

Feb. 10th 1860

Dear Riah

Your kind favor came to hand a few days since. I was very glad (as usual) to hear from home. Glad to hear that all was well. In your letter you said that you had had another attack. but had gotten over it but you still seem to be in low spirits: but you must cheer up you must travel about and enjoy yourself more do not think that you are about to die when there is nothing of consequence the matter with you.

There is nothing of interest in the city just now; today it is quite cold. Tobe Reamey got here day before yesterday. he Thomas and Dr. Semple came to our room as soon as they got here: (Dr. Simple and Tobe got here on the same day.) but not finding us in as we were all at the quiz left their cards and after supper Harry and I went to the Exchange to see them.

Tobe is a buster as fat as he can be and one of the finest looking men I ever saw. he was looking for Lucy today to go back with him but the train has come without her. I don't know whether he will wait any longer or not I expect that he will start tonight. he gave Harry a check for 190 dollars and a suit of clothes that cost 50 dollars which suited Harry very well–Tell Father that our rail road bill passed the senate today without any difficulty The appropriation that they made was 350,000 dollars: we will have a railroad now in a hurry. Thomas seems to be very well pleased. he smiles on both sides of his mouth.

Old Mr. Armstrong came down with Dr. Semple and last night at the theatre I thought he would kill himself laughing - he enjoyed himself finely it is the first time he ever was out of the county mightily pleased with Richmond says that he will go to New York next winter.

It will take him a month to tell what he saw in the theatre. he went back home this morning he would not stay longer. I was around a few nights ago at the Baptist institute to a grand consort, fine music and beautiful ladies, one of the schoolgirls gave me a ticket. You were asking me about the puppy you may have it if you want it I will pay for it when I come home. Tell Father that I would like to have a little money by the 20th of this month. I shall not start home before the 25th I don't recon Thos speaks of coming home about the 18th of this month but as the lectures hold on until the 27th I shall not start so soon

You must excuse this short letter as I am in a hurry to get it to the office before it closes
give all my highest regards
I remain your affectionate brother Ed

Richmond, Virginia
Nov, 8th 1860

Dear Sister

I was very glad a few days since to receive a letter from you, and hope that you will write oftener, and tell Dink and Moss to write to me also for you all have more time to write than I do. Be sure to tell them to write to me soon and give me all the news. There is nothing new in the city. There was a man hung here on last Friday he shot his sister in law because she refused to remarry with him.

Dr. Gibson operated on a little child today for osteosarcoma of the lower jaw he had to remove it or one half of it the child was very small about the size of Ellis.

The operation was a very savior one and I am very sorry to say this she died under the operation. Though it was as well done as I ever saw one of the sort she died from shock. She was too small for so large an operation, There is a good deal of excitement in the city about the election. This state has gone for Bell by a very small majority not more than two or three hundred. Lincoln is elected and some of the southern states are finding for disunion. There is germinating a panic in the money market here everybody is complaining of the scarcity of money some of the factories have discharged their hands and all produce is selling for as good as nothing. Great many merchants wish that they were out of business. The postscript in your letter was a charge not to sell his tobacco too soon. I reckon that before this you will have seen the bill of sale and have heard my reasons for selling so soon. I have seen since then that I did right in selling for the market is worse now than it was then and I don't suppose that it will be any better this winter. You all advised me not to sell until after the election but I saw very plainly that Lincoln would be elected and I knew that it would create fuss and excitement all over the South so I thought it would be better to sell before the election. It's true that it brought very little but I thought that I was doing the best and I believe so yet. Tell Father that I will be very economical and try to bring him as much of it back as I can but if he needs it before I return, let me know and I will send it to him. I am very sorry that uncle Tommy has pestered him about that money but if I were in his place I would not put myself to any trouble to pay him.

We are all very well at this time. I have enjoyed fine health this winter thus far and I hope that I may continue to enjoy the same. Let me know if Father has gotten over his rheumatism, how did Sallie enjoy her trip to the city. She seemed to suffer so much unease about Starley that I fear she did not enjoy it much. Tell Missy that I will send her more music if she will write and let me know what pieces she wants. I called on two very nice ladies a few evenings ago; Miss Pemberton & Miss Machins (?) Miss Pemberton is a very nice lady, Miss M also but she is so ugly but she has plenty of money.

My love to all, Write soon
Yours in haste
George Waller

June 20, 1861
Camp Pryor 3 miles from Manassas Junction

My Dearest Sallie,

Your hasty letter written on the 17th, arrived here about ten minutes ago, together with several others from Henry Co. I sorry to find that you once again thought that I have forgotten you, Sallie, surely you were not thinking of what you were writing when you penned that letter.

I tried to write to you, but I could not from Lynchburg. How could I forget you, the only woman I've ever loved. I will never forget you, the love I pledged 12 years ago at our bridal is as yet entirely yours. The flames burn more brightly than ever in your husband's heart.

I should have written from Lynchburg, but if you only knew the thousands of questions I've had to answer each day, or the things I've had to attend to connected with this company.

We have had no fight as of yet, look for one shortly at Alexandria, 27 miles distant. Our present camp is called Camp Pryor, have not yet seen Beauregard, though he is said to be at Manassas. I was there yesterday, it was a horribly hot and very nasty place. I dined with Col. Withers, Capt. Gravely and lieut. Smith, Buford of the Danville Grays and Capt. Clayborne of the Grays.

Charles Irving just left for the junction today. Major Early arrived here last night, he is Col. Of the regiment now.

Dr. Semple is here, he is a sort of hospital steward, attending the sick and superintends the medicine department of the hospital which is as yet a mere shanty.

I would like to get George in here, we could sure use his help.

John is the quartermaster of our company, he rips and roars about wasting food, much as usual.

It is awfully hot here in the middle of the day, but cools down at night.

John and I have been a little sick lately but not much.

The land here is very poor and the people don't have much interest for the war. We see few people, and those we do are from very common stock.

At Manassas there were about 15,000 men, well drilled and ready for a fight. About 299 were killed or disabled at the bridge near here the other day, you will see some accounts of it in the paper I suppose.

Darling what more can I say, think that while mountains may rise between us and rivers divide us, our eyes may see the stars in the sky. And our prays may ascend to the same father in heaven.

Pray for us Sallie, that we may be spared to see you all again.

Oh that I could this night clasp you to my bosom, Oh that I could see our little darlings, kiss them for me and give my love to Sooky, Perk, Dock, Joannah and all the negroes.

Bill is fat and fine and sends his love, he want to hear from home.

Darling, good night.
P. R. Reamey

Camp Pryor
July 28th 1861

Dear Mother

    Today being Sunday and also the first opportunity I have had to give you anything like a succinct account of the various scenes through which I have lately passed. I have concluded to avail myself of the opportunity and write you a letter not that I can give you anything new but merely my own experience of things that lately passed.

    On Wednesday week we left this place for some place we did not know where but of one thing we were certain that is that we were going to meet the enemy before we came back. Col. Early told us that we would have certainly to fight and in a short time as the enemy were advancing and had to be driven back and he expected us to do our share of the fighting of which he was going to give us a chance. We left camp and took up our line of march for some place about 2 ½ or 3 miles below here from which we could see the smoke rising from the burning bridges which our troops had burned in their retreat before the enemy

    We stayed all night in that place and early next morning we took up the line of march for a position on the Railroad thinking that they would come up the road where we were drawn out in line of battle and rested on our arms for about two hours when we were again started towards bull run and marched about 1 mile and ambushed in a thicket of pines We had not been long in our place of concealment when we saw a small smoke arise and in a few seconds heard the report of a cannon and then another and another in succession and in a few minutes we were put in line and loaded our guns and took the line of march for the scene of action. We had *gone about ½ mile further when we saw Gen. Beauregard come out of a house which had that morning been deserted by the family. We had to march about 1/4 mile right in the face of their artillery which was all the time belching forth its missiles of death and destruction. We were filed behind a pine thicket and the enemy thinking that our position had been changed from where we were began to fire at the house and orchard in which Gen. B was and one ball struck the kitchen and made the old fellow move his quarters.*

You can't imagine what strong feelings crept over me when the first two or three cannon balls came whistling by. They make a noise something like the noise of vile Ducks flying Well as I said we were behind the pines and the enemy trying to find us out firing balls and bomb shells in every direction but did not dream of our position In the mean time several regiments had moved down to the ford of the creek at which the enemy were trying to cross and when they came down to cross our men gave them a volley of musketry which told us that the fight had begun in earnest. I had read a good deal of the rattle of musketry and roar of artillery but of all the noises that are strange and ominous they are the most horrible. Just imagine a large wood of giant oakes all falling at the same moment and you have it as nearly as any thing I can think of and it is almost impossible to tell thunder and canon apart when the volleys follow in quick succession. The musketry had not been going on long when we saw the ambulances bearing off the wounded and dying from the field That was a sight to make the blood run cold in the stoutest heart some with their arms lost . . . some with a ball through the leg and some with their heads taken nearly off and in fact every imaginable place that you could imagine. We were marched down to the creek and that in a double quick time which is a run and it one of the hottest days you ever saw too and all the way along we were meeting the dead and wounded Those of the wounded who could talk were telling us to hurry up and give the rascals a thrashing. One fellow said, Boys and when you get there just hollow and they will run And there was more truth than poetry in it for our men would run down to the edge of the water where the Yankees were trying to cross and give a yell and fire into them when they would retreat and rally and come again but our men were too much for them and they had to retreat at last Though compelled to retreat we did not follow for they had a trap laid for us which would have cut us all to pieces by means of masked batteries. This was the fight on Thursday and on Sunday the big battle was fought. Although on Thursday and Sunday also we got none of the Glory of the victory for we did not get a single shot Yet we were subject to the fires of the enemy all the time and were in as much danger as almost any Sunday we laid all day under the heaviest kind of fire from their artillery in a perfect rain of bombs, balls and grape shot The bombs were bursting over our heads all the time

Our killed was on Thursday 8 killed and about 30 wounded of which 8 men died The enemy lost about 100 killed and as many more wounded

I must close by saying good by
White

Assuming 1861 as he recounts July 21st conflict 1st Manassas Jct.

Camp Ellis, Sep 7th

Dear Mother

As I have this headache today and do not feel like drilling I have concluded to address you another letter as I understand the other one I wrote you gave you so much pleasure and I assure you that there is nothing which I would not do to give you pleasure were it but for one moment.

There has been a considerable skirmish between our troops and the enemy near Masons Hill in which we got the best of the bargain running them about a mile.

I can think of nothing much to write about so I will give you some idea of the sufferings of the soldiers wounded in the battle of 21st July. I never saw many of them but a Lieutenant in the Patrick Co who was at the Junction the day of the battle and for several days after. Some had their arms shot off some with their legs mangled Horribly. He said that in rear of the hospital was a large pile of arms, legs, hands, feet and various parts of the body which had been cut off and thrown out. They were taken and carried down in the meadow and buried. One poor fellow who had been struck in the thy by a canon ball laid and suffered till the maggots got to working in his wound. he deliberately got up and hopped to the place where they kept their medicine and got a bottle of spirits of Turpentine and poured some of it in the wound which made the maggots travel to other quarters. he offered some to a yankee prisoner by his side but the yankee would (page 2) have nothing to do with it and eventually died from fear of being killed by some trick of the noble southern soldier. One poor fellow who had his arm and shoulder carried or torn off by a canon ball. He knew that he had to die. Taking his arm and shaking it by the hand he bid it an affectionate farewell and told them to bury it with him. He started to give some directions about letting his mother know of his death when he suddenly ceased to breathe and I do not know whether his mother was written to or not to let her know of her only sons death. He was her only son and she a widow but when the war broke out with true Spartan courage she buckled on his armor and bid him go forth to fight for his country and Spartan like either to return on his shield or with it. Surely such mothers have a place in history and the land that produces such mothers and such sons can not be conquered or subjugated.

I think there will be a terminus put to the war by the northern people by the end of next summer - I understand that the large quantities of soldiers in Washington have volunteered, not as soldiers but as citizen defenders of the capital. If such is the state of affairs at the North and I believe it the prospects of a lengthened war are very slim. I hope such is the true state of the case for if it is they will very quickly get tired of defending the capitol and it will be an easy (?) to Southern bravery. War is a very tiresome waste. It is so dull and monotonous, being the same round of duties day after day, week after week and month after month.

You would I expect be surprised to see me now

I weigh I reckon about 145. I am as fat as a bear and am (page 3) getting as strong as a young mule. I can eat more than any body you ever saw of my size. The fellows are always laughing at my eating so much but I am perfectly willing for them to laugh so long as I keep my health and grow fat. I have always wished to be a large man and there is now a very fair prospect for it. We have elected Hardain Dyer Captain of the Co. in place of Peter. He seems like he is going to make a very good officer. A good many of the fellows here were continually finding fault with Peter. But they are of the self conceited class who wanted Peter to pay very particular attention to them and who are dissatisfied with every thing. Also a good many are fawning upon Capt. Dyer for his favor by representing how much better off they are now than they were under Peter's administration. But Capt Dyer will very soon find that the same men will be complaining of him. Those who complain most too are the very men to whom Peter was most lenient and showered most of his favour upon. At the head of whom stands Jno. L. Hamlett. If Peter ever does another favor for Jno Hamlett he ought to be kicked out of all respectable society. A man who has vilified him and slandered him in every manner he can. And is now trying to ruin Peters character by circulating reports that he believed Peter had used up all the money given to the Co. Happily Geo. Hairston kept all the funds of the Co. And Peter I think had nothing to do with it but to give an order upon Isom to those men who were entitled to it.

This Noble Co. The Henry Guards have deceived me some and I must acknowledge more than I expected. For there are a good many very mean lowlifed men in it whilst upon the contrary there are some very high toned high minded honorable men in the Co. You need never believe any report to Peters discredit coming from any quarter. For Peter I know treated Harry and myself with more harshness than any one else except John Reamey because he did not want to appear partial. And I have no cause for complaint nor has any one else but upon the contrary had great cause to be gratified. And the only fault I could find too familiar with his men. And there are a good many men in the Co who are of that class who respect a man only when he keeps aloof from them. Who are like a gang of dogs and are continually snarling and growling among themselves *and the only way to be safe from their attacks is to keep our of their reach.*

As I have nearly finished this sheet I must draw my letter to a close by saying good by till next time.

*Give my love to everybody and in your prayers remember
Your Son White*

Bivouack Near Fredericksburg Va
December 4, /62

Dear Ria

    Your last came to hand the other night and I was very much surprised to learn that you all had not received any letters from me lately for I have written 3 or 4 since we got to Culpepper. I have no news to write a fight is expected here every day though I must say I don't think there will be any fight here shortly and I do not think there will be any more fighting on this line till next summer. Then there will be a tremendous fight which will end the War. Rumors of foreign intervention are still rife in camp but I don't see as yet anything reliable and don't put any faith in any of them. I understand that there is no evidence against Jack Heath whatever. Cards (?) are still going night and day without any intermission whatever. How did father come to employ Bauseman. I thought he was coming back to the Army. I only made $12.1/2 on the Barrel of Apples for my share Joe Rea made the same amount. The weather is pretty cold here now but continues clear Every two or three days the weather looks like rain but the wind gets in the north and it clears off again. Tell Big Lew he must be more careful with the axes next time and that I hope the squirrel skins will get more tender but I am afraid he does not hit them plum every time.

    What is the reason that Spot Redd does not come back to the Company He and his crowd have all been ordered back to the Company but don't come. I have just heard of the death of Tom West who died at Liberty a few days ago. Tom made a good soldier and I am sorry to hear of his death Well so ends all things human. I have been very fortunate during this war in having my health and having *the eye of Providence on me all the time in guarding my life during battle and disease in camp. I will finish as soon as I come off of drill*

Well Drill is over and I must conclude. Our tents have been sent after for us to winter in

I would like very much to get a furlough home during the winter but I have no idea of getting one.

Col. Hairston could not get a furlough. He might try to get me one through his influence with his superior influence. But his influence is not very great and even if it was it won't hardly do anything with the officers of this division . . . Ed says send his boots by the first person coming. I told him that you all would have sent them long ago if you could have found any body coming down here to bring them. You all can't imagine (who never felt it) what going barefooted is

Well give my love to everybody and write soon to your Brother, White

P.S. Hardain send his love to all of you.

Bivouack Near Fredricksburg, Virginia
December 6/62

Dear Sallie

Yesterday brought Mrs. Farley and a letter from you and like everything from home was read with . Yesterday it commenced hailing raining and snowing until this morning the sun is shining in all his brilliancy upon snow about one or two inches thick.

You will be surprised to learn that the confederacy is nearly played out in the eating line. We have had nothing to eat since yesterday morning but a few crackers and only five of them to a man for a days rations When we get beef it only makes one meal

Well the Yankees are as bad off as we are so their deserters say some of those who deserted say that they are getting almost nothing to eat and that they are almost naked and barefooted and that they will give an overcoat for a plug of Tobacco anywhere and that thousands would desert if they

While I am thinking of it Tell Peter to see Jack Heath and get my overcoat from him and if he has sold it make him pay $2 for it. I reckon he knows the coat. The one Mrs. Bullington made for me last fall. Tell him to keep the coat till I come home or he can send it to me. Ed says you can send the coats by Old Joe Jones of Reid Creek who is going to come down shortly. We are all well and will probably keep so if we can get something to eat. Give my best respects to Miss Lulie Bucktrout and the widow.

Hairston sends his respects to all of you
Give my love to every body and kiss all the children for me
and write soon to your brother
White

Camp 24th Va Infty
Clark Co., VA June 23rd 1863

Dear Sister,

I embrace this leisure to let you know my where about. After days of hard marching through dust & the oppressive sun we have gained this point, which you can see from the map is between Winchester & Harpers Ferry- we have been resting two days.

We had some very hot weather to march in many fell on the wayside with sunstroke & syncope Some died, others recovered and came up. (Co H) was the only company that stood up to the march. It did not have a single man to fall out. It is now considered one of the best companies in the regt.

White came very near fainting, but I found him & took his gun & put his baggage in the ambulance & then he got on very well. Peter Waller fell on the wayside. I bathed his head, gave him a drink of brandy & that night he came up. It was the hardest march we have ever had.

We are all well now & expect to go into Maryland in a few days. We have had several cavalry fights in Loudon in the last few days. I think that the Yankees are trying to find out where our troops are. Stewart captured a currier of Hookers the other day with dispatches to Gen. Stoneman to press on to this gap of the mountain & hold it at all hazards but we got here before he did so we held it instead of the Yankees. Gen. Ewell's corps is in Maryland. I suppose you have heard of our victory at Winchester. Old Milroy escaped.

When we get in Yankeedom, I intend to have anything that is good, & I shall try to bring you something back with me if I keep my health. We are going to lead the Yankees a hard road this summer. We have got the men to whip the scamps & we will surely do it.

We are now in the Shenandoah valley. It is the finest country I ever saw. I do wish that you could see it. We all had quite a spree the other day, wading the river, it was about waist deep, & I never saw men enjoy anything more.

Spot Redd & myself, took a walk out yesterday evening & struck up with an old gentleman that invited us to supper with him & you know that we did not refuse, although I had been to supper. He entertained us very kindly & besides he had a lovely daughter which was very interesting & it devolved upon me to interest her in conversation which I found a very easy & pleasant task, she being well posted upon the general topics of the day & very affluent, we sat with them until bed time. They insisted upon our staying all night & they pressed us to call & see them again. I had a pet squirrel which I gave the young lady for which she was very thankful, she named it after me & seemed very much gratified . . . but I must close.

White & I are very well.
My love to all
write soon to your affect brother
Geo E. Waller

Hanover Co Va
Taylorsville Depot
Sept. 28th 1863

Dear Sister,

We are again, deprived of our good Quarters. We came up here night before last. We hated to quit our good cabins at Chaffins Farm very much but must obey orders, which this regt. has never refused to do yet. I don't know how long we may stay here. I hope we may go back soon.

While I was in Richmond to take the cars I saw a paroled prisoner from this Regt who had left a few evenings before, he told me that White was getting on very well. had gotten so that he could hobble about on crutches, said that he did not suffer for but one thing & that was chewing Tobacco. They can get but little & that is very indifferent.

He said that White had confederate money but it was worth nothing to him, he said that he had 13 dollars in green backs, which he gave White when he left. He says that White will come as soon as he is able which will be about one month he thinks.

I wrote White as much as I could cram on one page a few days before I left the other camp.

There is no news at this place worth relating. Jim Banister is at home with Capt Barrow at this time. Bring me anything that you all desired to send & he is a very trusty boy & will bring anything through safely. If he don't call for the boxes, direct them to me the care of A S Buford Va State agent Richmond Va but I suppose Jim will call for them. Tell Mother not go to any trouble about clothes for me as I can get plenty from the Government. I shall want my Boots

I could get a furlough but am waiting thinking probably White will get back & I can see you all together.

They were giving one pint of unsalted meat and a quarter pound of bacon per day. The bacon is usually eaten raw. To fry it would have caused it to shrink too much. made from parched wheat, rye or sometimes rice.

Nothing more my love to all excuse bad writing, as it is done on my knee

Write soon & often to your affect brother.
Geo.
I will write more next time

Near Smithfield, N.C.
March 7th 1864

Dear Sister,

I shall drop you a few lines merely to let you know where & how I am. We are now 30:ty miles below Wilmington at a little place called Smithfield. We had a very pleasant trip to this place- from Goldsboro to Wilmington we came by rail & from there here we came on Steam Boats It was a beautiful trip down the Cape Fear River The grandest scenery I ever witnessed. I could see the billows on the ocean rising like mountains & looking as white as cotton & away in the distance the masts of ships were visible. supposed to be the blockading fleet. We have got to go ten or twelve miles below here to take charge of a fort of heavy guns so they will convert us into artillery to shoot at the Yankee vessels.

This is the most barren country I ever saw with but one recommendation that is a plenty of oysters & fish. I fear if we stay here long we will have a plenty of sickness. There is smallpox here now & in the fall they have yellow fever & cholera.

A good many vessels run in & out of the blockade here. Three came in while we were at Wilmington & there is one lying in the River now to run out. She has seven hundred bales of cotton on board

I will write at more length as soon as I can
Write soon
Geo E. Waller

I had to close on the other side to pull a tooth for Capt Bentley. Harding got to us while we were at Kinston. He brought my box all right & we are now enjoying mothers ham & were it not for it we would have no bacon I wish that you all had some of the oysters & clams that we have If you will look on the map you can see where we are we are in Brunswick county as soon as we get in permanent camp I will write a long letter & give you all the points. I think it probable that we will stay here all the summer-

Harding Dyer was elected Lieut. in Co. H this morning he had no opposition. Maj. Hambrick & many of the company wanted me to run for the office but!!I did not want it.

You all must write often for it will take a long time for the letters to get here

good by,
Very truly your brother
Geo E Waller

Camp near Goldsboro N.C.
March 30*th* 1864

Dear Rita

    Your letter containing Whites & Hamletts notes came to hand a few days since. I was delighted to hear from them and was quite surprised to here that White was not yet well of his wound. I hope that if the exchange of Prisoners continues he may soon get home where he may soon get well. I wish I was at home so that I could assist in sending his cloths & money to him though I think that "Flag of Truce" is a very uncertain - as all things have to be inspected by Yankees & you know their thievish propensities-

    This morning. I was very glad to get away from Fort Caswell & I think that most all the Regt was glad to get off. We came up here to meet Gen Burnside who has landed with 12 thousand troops. I have heard nothing from him since we got here I hope that he may not come any farther in to the country, for I don't want to do any fighting yet.- I here that Sam Fontaine Jim & John Redd have gone to "Drurys Bluff". I suppose that Peter Davis will follow suit. Co H was very glad to get rid of Louts Fontaine & Davis- Frank Powell (page 2) and Harding Dyer were elected to fill their places both of which will make good officers. I think they will go in fights which Davis & Fontaine never would do. Tell Mass that I sent her box of shells by express to Danville. Directed it to her in care of stage agent. She must tell the stage driver to call at the express office & get it for her. Enclosed you will find the receipt which I took for it.

    It is strange that White has never mentioned any of my letters. he certainly did not get them I send Whites & Hamletts notes back.. probably you may need them for reference We are now camped in our old camp don't know how long we will stay nor where we will *go when we move- my health is very good at this time though I have reduced very much in flesh one of Co H is very much complaining this morning I fear that he is taking smallpox . . . symptoms very much like it. - As I am not in humor to write this morning you will excuse this short note- my love to all Had a very hard rain yesterday & its cloudy & cool this morning - are they catching any fish in trap this spring.*

very affectionately yours
Geo E. Waller

Picketts Field Infirmary
Chester Oct 7th 1864

Dear Sallie

Your letter came to hand some time since and should have answered sooner but!! I was taken sick just as I received it. I had a slight attack of Bilious Remittent Fever, was laid up 5 or 6 days. I am now well again & hope I may have no more of the malarias diseases. These Bilious Headaches are very severe. My Regt are suffering very much with the chills. I have about 60 here in Hospital now and no one to attend to them but myself.

Dr. Harrison is on a Board to examine in all the Hospitals & public workshops of every kind & send all able bodied men to the field & having no Asst Surgeon. Harrison's departure leaves me entirely alone with all the sick on my hands but I get on very well. Dr. Harrison will be gone I suppose all the winter, he has to go all over Virginia & North Carolina.

My Regt is on the North side of the James, had them in two fights & they have been fighting again today & I expect they have had them in again. it seems that when there is any fighting to be done they call for the 24th but I don't think they can fight it much more for it is very small now we had some of our best soldiers killed the other day. They will fight as long as there are any of them left.

I think that Grant will make a general attack shortly he has been receiving heavy reinforcements & he will do all in his power to gain success before the election so that the old "Ape" may be rushed into office again & if General Lee don't get some reinforcements I fear the result - Lee & his army will do all that any General can do with the same number but!! There is such a thing as being overpowered. The army of N.V.A. has been very much reduced by casualties this summer. but!! if Gen Lee can get twenty thousand fresh troops all will be well. I would not be suppressed any day for Grant to pitch his worthless hirelings against every man that is able to stand behind breastworks & fire a gun should press to Lees assistance one month will end the campaign and with it (I hope) the war. but!! if we are overpowered & Grant gain success who can say how long this cruel & bloody conflict may last. Gen Price or ("old dad") as he is more familiarly known in his own command) is sweeping everything before him Yankees very much excited in St. Louis I wish we had his troops here for the protection of Richmond. Things are working well everywhere The only place I have any fears for is this army I fear is not strong enough to contend with such numbers as Grant will mass on us but let us hope for the best and do all that is in our power.

There is nothing new or interesting in camp. we are having beautiful weather. I am anxious to see some heavy frost just to stop the chills. John & Peter Waller got a fine box from home the other day & invited me down & I tell you I enjoy so the good apples & brandy. some of the finest Bucking ham I ever saw. Billy King's health is as good as usual if anything I believe it is better. I fear that his lungs will fail when the weather gets cold & damp, especially if we have to march any during the winter. I have not heard from Aunt Peggy for a long time. I have a notion to write to the old lady to have me a nice frock coat made for winter. don't you recon she would do it. I believe she would especially if I make her believe that I am coming to see Miss Jones as soon as opportunity offers.

How is Peter & the children- Starley shooting squirrels Peter practicing Physic, &cc how did your crop of corn turn out, I recon Father will make a good crop of corn. By the by, how comes on The Tableaux I am sorry Miss Antionette left so you could not carry them out. Frank Graveley & Sallie Hughes I understand are the most loving couple ever seen- & Mariah & old blind Bill are very much attached to each other. Tell the Dr if he gets tired (anytime this winter) of staying about home, to come down & spend a few days with me I will give him good quarters & the best table I can raise-

My love to all.
Write soon to your affect..brother.
Geo. E. Waller

PS Direct to me at Chester, & I will get it much sooner. It's reported this evening that we retook Fort Harrison today

Chester
Oct 23rd 1864

Dear Sallie

It though it is Sunday I shall attempt a reply to your letter of the 17th, which came to hand a few days since. I am always glad to get your letters for you give me more points than any other correspondent I have in Henry. I feel very well this evening having eaten a hearty dinner so you may expect a short & dull letter. There is really nothing in camp to write about, here at the Hospital we have the same routine of duty every day. My list of sick has very much diminished recently. I haven't more than 15 or 20 on hand now. I am still alone with everything to do myself. I cure them & send them back nearly as fast as they come; some nights I get rather lonesome. Dennis comes around about every other night.

Last night he & I sat up until eleven oclock talking over old times as they were before the war, and from that we got on matrimony and our prospects of marrying what type of beauty we admired most. Dennis related all of his love scrapes from first to last which occupied some time. he has almost come to the conclusion that he is never to marry but!! I shall hope on yet. shall look on the bright side for of all thing the life of an old bachelor is the most unenviable I think. I have ever looked on it with perfect horror & yet there has been an impression on my mind for a long time that it would be my fate despite all my powers. I hope it may be but a delusion I place such a high estimate on myself that I fear I shall never find a lady that will suit me in every respect. The lady that marries me must have all accomplishments that make females attractive. I hope when the South shall be once more free and independent that I may be able to find some fair damsel of some of the southern who may possess besides my heart, about one hundred thousand dollars. Then I shall whisper the softest words of love & affection & if possible win her heart as well as her money. You must not conclude from my talk that I would marry any lady for money alone. (it shall be no objection) but I would not marry any lady that I could not love if she had untold wealth. but why talk & reason I thus: when this war is upon us & who can tell when it will stop. Early gets whipped every time he fights. The Yankee cavalry are so strong they flank him out of position & catch his artillery. If the Yankees want a whipping let them try Gen Lee & his veterans & I will insure them that some of them will get their "new cloth torn" (camp slang) We rather expect an attack from the ruffians every night but we are ready for them, so let them come whenever they feel disposed we have a large quantity of lead & Iron waiting to give them a reception. Butlers canal is supposed to be nearly done & then we expect a general attack from both land & water but they will find the road to Richmond very hard to travel even on water.

Sam Fretwell has just been in to see me sends his respects to you & family he is in Hospital with Chronic Diarrhea, looks rather badly but is still the same boy as he was when you knew him. Capt Barrow has just come in to stay all night with me he is going to Richmond in the morning to see who is staying at Chimborazo Hospital his leg is well but has not got its use yet.

You were enquiring if we had had any frost, we have had frost for two weeks & yes tardy we had wind rain & snow. That beats you. Tell Peter not to kill old Parker, we will make a soldier of him next spring. All the Governors are in convention down south now considering the propriety of putting negroes in the army. Old Parker will do very well to catch the ball that might kill some good man. Why did you send the money for pen points. you know I will send them without it. enclosed you will find it returned spend it for something else. I shall send the points as soon as I can get them & that will be as soon as I can go down to the Q.M. Dept. such things never cost me anything Capt. Woods or Sgt Hale will give me as many as I want in the next letter I will send you 6 points which will last you a while & as to the coat I know you haven't the cloth to spare you have a heap of little ones to cloth so you keep your cloth. You will need it all I have written to Granma to have me one made & I think she can refuse. if she does I shall write her a letter. Tell Peter if he want anything of mine the way of clothing that is at home just to help himself. Probably he may want some of those flannel shirts. I saw George & Granma's Oliver as they passed going to Petersburg to work on the fortifications. They were very glad to see someone they knew so far from home seemed to be in fine spirits.

I must close as it is now dark & this is longer now than interesting. I was very glad you reproved me for spelling so badly. I always was a bad hand at the business. I hope you may correct me every time. I expect you will find many words spelt wrong in this.

My love to Peter & all the children
write soon to
Geo E. Waller

MAJOR BATTLES OF THE TWENTY-FOURTH VIRGINIA INFANTRY

Manassas, July 21, 1861

Williamsburg, May 5, 1862

Second Manassas, August 28–30, 1862

Sharpsburg, September 17, 1862

Fredericksburg, December 13, 1862

Gettysburg, July 1–3 1863

Petersburg, June 9, 1864–March 25, 1865

Sailor's Creek, April 6, 1865

Appomattox Court House, April 9, 1865

Notes

Siblings

George's twelve brothers and sister, only five (including George) survived to adulthood:

01.	Mariah (Riah) Louisa	03/1831 – 08/1898 (67 years)
02.	Sarah (Sallie) Jane	03/1833 – 05/1866 (33 years)
03.	Mary Eliza	03/1835 – 02/1897 (62 years)
04.	John Stephen	10/1837 – 11/1837 (1 month)
05.	George Edmund	10/1838 – 02/1915 (76 ½ years)
06.	Samuel Gallatin	12/1840 – 04/1864 (23 ½ years) exact date 04/05/1864
07.	Judith Ann Malinda	03/1843 – 01/1919 (76 years)
08.	William (White) Duncan	05/1845 – 01/1865 (19 ½ years) exact date 01/28/1865
09.	Albert Randolph	12/1848 – 09/1850 (20 months)
10.	Elizabeth	? (presumably stillborn)
11.	Lewis Skidmore	09/1851 – 03/1927 (75 ½ years)
12.	John	? (presumably stillborn)
13.	James	? (presumably stillborn)
14.	Winston	? (presumably stillborn)

Thirteen brothers and sisters: Mariah Louisa (Riah), Sarah (Sallie), Mary Eliza, John Stephens, Samuel G., Judith, William Duncan (White), Albert R., Lewis S., Elizabeth, John, James, and Winston.

These are Dr. Waller's siblings. Wm. Duncan Waller is the one in the letters.

Name	Birth	Death
Mariah Louisa Waller	29 MAR 1831	16 AUG 1898
Daughter	Henry County, VA	Henry County VA
Sallie Jane Waller	16 MAR 1833	15 MAY 1866
Daughter	Henry County, VA	Henry County, VA
Mary Eliza Waller	21 MAR 1835	18 FEB 1897
Daughter	Henry County, VA	Henry County, VA
John Stephen Waller	19 OCT 1837	18 NOV 1837
Son	Henry County, VA	Henry County, VA
George Edmund Waller	17 OCT 1838	2 FEB 1915
Son	Henry County, VA	Henry County, VA
Samuel Gallatin Waller	5 DEC 1840	5 APR 1864
Son	Henry County, VA	Henry County, VA
Judith Ann Malida Waller	20 MAR 1843	2 JAN 1919 Hints (2)
Daughter	Henry County, VA	Washington DC
William Duncan Waller	12 MAY 1845	28 JAN 1865 Hints (2)
Son	Henry County, VA	
Albert Randolph Waller	30 DEC 1848	3 SEPT 1850 Hint (1)
Son	Henry County, VA	
Lewis Skidmore Waller	15 SEP 1851	12 MAR 1927
Son	Henry County, VA	Leaksville, Rockingham County, NC

Points of interest:

George E. Waller

October 17, 1838 – was born in Henry County, Virginia

1861 – graduated Richmond County, Virginia, USA Medical College of Virginia Commonwealth University School of Medicine, Richmond; Hampden-Sidney Coll. Med. Dept., 1861,

His service in the Confederate Army lasted exactly three years

March 17, 1862 – enlisted into Company H, Twenty-Fourth Regiment Virginia Infantry, formerly the Henry Volunteers at rank of private, later achieved rank of corporal

1863–1864 – served as hospital steward in charge of (Pickett's?) field hospital; he was praised as exceptionally competent and knowledgeable

February 1865 – fell ill with pneumonia

March 18, 1865 – was admitted to Chimborazo Hospital no. 3 with abscesses; he did not return to service after his illness

Postwar

1868 – he married Sarah Louise Putzel in 1868 in Martinsville, Virginia; he served as coroner for Henry County in Martinsville, Virginia, for many years

1890 – along with Stuart Hairston and assistant surgeon Dr. P. R. Reamey, formed the Confederate Veterans' Association; his wife

Sarah was instrumental in erecting a monument in Martinsville, the Confederate Dead Memorial, which stands today

February 2, 1915 – died in Henry County, Virginia, at seventy-six years of age

George had two brothers killed in the war, not much written about it in letters:

William Duncan Waller was born in 1845 in Martinsville, Virginia. William Duncan Waller died on January 28, 1865, when he was nineteen and half years old.

Samuel G. Waller was born in 1839 in Henry County, Virginia. Samuel G. Waller died on April 5, 1864, in Richmond County, Virginia, when he was twenty-three and half years old.

Dr. Peter Randolph Reamey and His Three Brothers

JTMartinonline.com/documents/civilwar.htm

Peter and his three brothers, Henry Clay Reamy, John Starling Reamy, and Daniel Webster Reamy, enlisted at the same time.

John died of wounds inflicted during First Manassas, sixteen days after, on 8/6/61, and was buried somewhere near the battlefield.

Henry, a hospital steward under Peter, was presumed to have been injured while treating John under enemy fire. Henry died on September 18, 1861, fifty-nine days after First Manassas, and was buried in Oakwood Cemetery in Henry County.

John's wife Elizabeth (Bettie) gave birth to John's youngest Samuel Hairston Reamy on December 1861, just four months after John Died. Later, the other brother, Daniel, married John's widow Bettie.

White mentioned in his letter dated 9/7/61 that Company H had replaced Peter and how Peter had never shown any of his kin favoritism, mentioning specifically John as well as one named Harry, who may refer to Henry.

Here is how I imagine it unfolded: After John died and was buried in the field, Peter realized that Henry would not survive his wounds either, so Peter and Daniel resigned from the military and carried Henry home to die and be properly buried and to care for John's widow.

BOOKS/REFERENCES

WEBSITES

http://www.civilwar.org

http://www History.mfrl.org content 24th Virginia.pdf

http://www hillstudioHenry-County-survey-reportfinal.com

http://www.worldcat.org/title/ george-e-waller-letters-1858-1864/oclc/27188741

http://www2.lib.unc.edu/mss/inv/w/Waller,George_E.html

Letters 1860, from George Waller to his parents in Henry County, Virginia, about his medical studies in Richmond. The remaining letters, 1861–1864, discuss the routines of camp life, battles, family news, and George Waller's observations as an assistant surgeon in the Twenty-Fourth Virginia Regiment, and, after July 1864, as a hospital steward with Pickett's field infirmary, Chester, Virginia letters from

Sam and White Waller, who was with George during the early part of the war, are also present.

http://www.perseus.tufts.edu/hopper

Richmond Times Dispatch

Letters from Camp Pryor, an Unknown Private
http://www.JTMartinonline.com/documents/civilwar.htm

Personal Genealogy Site for J. T. Martin Ancestors, Including Dr. Peter R. Reamey

http://www Hampton-Sidney College.org

"Once again, at the outset of war the student body organized a company, with the president as captain. These men, officially mustered as Company G, 20th Virginia Regiment, 'The Hampden-Sydney Boys,' saw action in the disaster of Rich Mountain 9-10 July 1861), were captured, and were paroled by General George B. McClellan on the condition that they return to their studies." (*My note*: George, wisely, did not go with them.)

BOOKS

Judith, P. A. (1976) *A History of Henry County, Virginia, with Biographical Sketches of Its Most Prominent Citizens and Genealogical Histories of Half a Hundred of Its Oldest Citizens.* Illustrated edition. Hill Regional Publishing.

Johnston, D. E. 1914. *The Story of a Confederate Boy in the Civil War, 1845–1917.*

Gunns, R. W. 1987. *Complete History of the 24th Virginia Infantry, The Virginia Regimental Series.* First edition. H>E> Howard, Inc., PO Box 4161, Lynchburg, Virginia 24502

Perry, T. D. Stoneman's Raid.

And many other reference books in my library

ACKNOWLEDGMENTS

Dr. Robert Massey
U.S. History Consultant
Arizona Historical Society
Virginia Historical Society
Vice President, Arizona Genealogical Advisory Board
National Genealogy Committee, SCV
Commander, Arizona Division, SCV
Past Lieutenant Commander, Arizona Division, SCV
Chairman, Arizona Division Sesquicentennial Committee, SCV
Genealogist, Arizona Division, SCV
Lieutenant Commander, Col. Sherod Hunter Camp No. 1525, SCV
Genealogist, Gen. John B. Magruder Chapter, MOSB
Sons of Union Veterans, Picacho Peak Camp No. 1

The Bassett Historical Center
Pat Ross, director operational manager and staff
3964 Fairystone Park Highway, Bassett, Virginia 24055

The Bassett Historical Center is the repository for all genealogical research and local history for the counties of Henry and Patrick and the city of Martinsville, Virginia.

Jon Willen, MD
Infectious disease specialist
Many thanks for his surgical knowledge of the time.

Peter J. D'Onofrio, Ph. D.
President
Society of Civil War Surgeons, Inc.
www.civilwarsurgeons.org

All physicians who serviced in the Confederacy in a medical capacity.
Courtesy of F. T. Hambrecht
Biographical register.

George Edmund Waller M.D.
1861- Graduated Medical College of Virginia at Richmond,
03/17/1862- Mustered in as Private 24th Virginia Inf.
04/24/1862 -Detailed as Hospital Steward, 24th Virginia Inf. Performed duties of an Asst. Surgeon, but no evidence he was appointed as an Asst. Surgeon.

Peter Randolph Reamey M.D.
1851- Graduated Medical College of Virginia, at Richmond,
071861-Capt. Co. H 24th Virginia Inf.

George Tucker Harrison M.D.
1856- Graduated University of Virginia, Charlottesville, Va.
05/22/1961 Appointed Asst. Surgeon, Virginia Forces by the Governor.
07/00/1861- Asst. Surgeon, 24th Virginia Infantry.
06/12/1863-Promoted Surgeon, 24th Virginia Infantry

James Semple M.D.
1856- Graduated from Jefferson Medical College, Philadelphia, Pa.
06/05/1861- Enlisted Co. H. 24th Virginia at Lynchburg, Va.
06/12/1861- Detailed as Hospital Steward.

John R Curd M.D.
1855- Graduated Jefferson Medical College, Philadelphia, Pa.
05/24/61- Enlisted Co. C at Lynchburg, Va. Detailed as Hospital Steward.
06/03/1861 - Asst. Surgeon.

Sterling Neblett Jr.
06/03/1861- F&S Surgeon

Jodi L. Koste
Archivist and head, Resources and Operations VCU, Libraries Faculty Vita
(Associate professor) Tompkins-McCaw Library

Mr. Ed W. Kuykendall of Martinsville, Virginia
Descendant of George and Sara Waller

Anne Bettis

And many thanks to **Anne Bettis,** a direct descendant of Dr. Peter Reamey and Sallie Waller Reamey, for her contribution of **Waller and Reamey letters**. She was invaluable to this work.

B. J. Wood, Writer and Author

For guiding me through the art of structuring a manuscript.

FINAL NOTES

PERSONAGES

STONEMAN'S RAID.
Thomas D. Perry

By April 1865, the war was about to come to an end. Until that time, Henry and Patrick Counties in Virginia were untouched by the armies of the United States of America. That changed as Robert E. Lee evacuated Richmond, the capitol of Virginia and the Confederate States of America. As Lee went west for a fateful meeting with Ulysses S. Grant to surrender his Army of Northern Virginia at Appomattox, Confederate President Jefferson F. Davis came south on the train to Danville.

At this same time, from the east came over four thousand cavalry under the overall command of Major General George Stoneman. General Stoneman attended the United States Military Academy at West Point in the heralded class of 1846, that also included George B. McClellan and George Pickett. During his third year, Stoneman's roommate was Thomas J. Jackson. He was not "Stonewall" yet. After graduating, the six-foot-four-inch Stoneman, described as a generous-hearted, whole-souled companion, was part of a march from Kansas to California in the Mormon Battalion during the Mexican War.

Stoneman himself did not come to Martinsville, but instead sent Brigadier General William J. Palmer, commanding a brigade of Stoneman's cavalry.

Shepherdstown, West Virginia, just a few days after the battle along Antietam Creek. Confederates sent Palmer to Castle Thunder Prison in Richmond, Virginia, suspected as a spy but later exchanged him in January 1863. He returned to his regiment in 1863 in Tennessee and served in the Tullahoma, Chickamauga, and Knoxville campaigns and in 1864 near Chattanooga.

On January 14, 1865, near Red Hills, Alabama, leading Company A of the Fifteenth Pennsylvania Cavalry, Palmer's actions led twenty-nine years later to his receiving the Medal of Honor bestowed upon him on February 24, 1894, stating: "With less than 200 men, attacked and defeated a superior force of the enemy, capturing their field piece and about 100 prisoners without losing a man."

During George Stoneman's raid, Palmer received an appointment as Brevet Brigadier General at age twenty-nine. Only George A. Custer became a general at a younger age. One commander said Palmer was worth "a whole brigade of most cavalry."

Col. William J. Palmer's first brigade of cavalry included the Tenth Michigan Cavalry Regiment under the command of Col. Luther Trowbridge, the Twelfth Ohio under Col. Robert H. Bentley, and the Fifteenth Pennsylvania under Lt. Col. Charles M. Betts.

On March 21, 1865, Stoneman left Mossy Creek, Tennessee, with 4,500 men. They reached Boone, North Carolina, on March

28th. The flooding Yadkin River separated Palmer's men, who crossed to the north side, from the remainder of the force on March 29th. On April 1st, the commands still divided by the Yadkin River reached Elkin on the north side of the river and Jonesville on the south side, respectively.

Stoneman reunited his entire command on the north side of the river in Surry County at Rockford on April 2nd. On April 3rd, Robert E. Lee and the Army of Northern Virginia evacuated Richmond and Petersburg.

Stoneman raided Mount Airy. A native of Surry County, James Gwyn commented on the Yankee raiders as they came by his place on the north side of the Yadkin: "The Yankees passed along on both sides of the river . . . Those who passed acted very well . . . Treatment of citizens by Palmer's Brigade on the north side of the river evoked the surprise of the residents who feared much harsher treatment."

As Abraham Lincoln walked the streets of Richmond with his youngest son, Stoneman moved to Christiansburg by midnight of April 4th–5th. Palmer's brigade destroyed railroad tracks of the Virginia and Tennessee Railroad east of Christiansburg. The journey to North Carolina came next and began on April 7th. The route led through Henry County. The direct route ran through Patrick County, where Stoneman and two brigades under the overall command of Alvin Gillem traversed.

On the return journey of Stoneman's command, Palmer came through Martinsville and Henry County fighting a battle along Jones Creek when he ran into 250 Confederate cavalry under the command of James T. Wheeler. General Gillem, in his report said, "Colonel Palmer, commanding the First Brigade had been directed to send the Tenth Michigan directly on the railroad to

Martinsville, by some misunderstanding he marched with his entire command."

General George Brown, in his record of service of Michigan volunteers in the Civil War, wrote that: "The regiment moved at 4 a.m. and by a forced night march reached Henry Court House about 7 a.m. of the 8th, to find it occupied by about 500 of Wheeler's Cavalry."

Based on this description and the location of the skirmish on Jones Creek north of Martinsville, the encampment appears to have been established in the deep, steep-side valley between the railroad tracks and Commonwealth Boulevard today. Stillhouse Branch flows in this valley to empty into Jones Creek. Wheeler's Confederate troops took refuge there after receiving an attack by Capt. James H. Cummins and a battalion of the Tenth Michigan Cavalry.

An account from the Tenth Michigan Cavalry states: "Captain James H. Cummins, commanding the leading battalion, immediately charged and routed the party in the town, and drove them back on the main body. The noise of the firing aroused the main body, which quickly saddled and formed, and when Cummins reached them, they were in line of battle. Nothing could restrain the Tenth, however, and they attacked with vigor, and the enemy was driven out of the woods. They mainly took refuge in a deep depression so common at the South, and there, huddled together, they formed an excellent target for the Spencer carbines of Captain Dunn and his plucky boys. The casualties of the enemy were reported as 27 killed."

The result was on the Union side, there were five killed, including a sergeant and lieutenant. T. C. Kenyon, "a noble young man" of the Tenth Michigan Cavalry and four others were killed.

The dead rested in the Episcopal church yard, now Baptist, at the corner of Church and Moss Streets in Martinsville until reburial at the National Cemetery in Danville.

Col. James T. Wheeler wrote on April 8th, twelve miles east of Henry Court House: "The enemy attacked me at 7 a.m. today after a spirited fight were repulsed with severe loss on his side. The force which attacked me was 800 strong." Jefferson Davis, in Danville, wrote on April 9th, of the fight to Robert E. Lee: "The enemy cavalry reported in small force at Henry Court House yesterday. Colonel Wheeler engaged them with about half their force say with 250 men and checked them."

Palmer stayed in Martinsville (apparently in a home at 33 Church Street), and Wheeler withdrew twelve miles from town.

Wheeler wrote later on April 8th: "At dark tonight the enemy was still in Henry Court House. During the day, he was re-enforced by about 800. They tell citizens that they will advance on Danville in the morning. As yet no buildings have been burned."

Instead, Palmer rejoined Stoneman's command on April 9th in Danbury, North Carolina. He did not know that Jefferson Davis was a few miles away in Danville. Stoneman's raid continued down into Piedmont, North Carolina, attacking Salisbury on April 12th. Stoneman returned to Tennessee four days later. Palmer continued in pursuit of Jefferson Davis. Stoneman left Gillem in command of the rest of his force. Gillem moved through Morganton, and Rutherford, where he sacked Asheville and returned to Tennessee on April 26th.

On May 10, Union cavalry captured President Davis near Irwinville, Georgia. Two days later, the Confederates won the last battle of the war near Brownsville, Texas.

Dr, Peter Randolph Reamy
12 Jan 1829-24 years old
Courtesy of Pat Ross, Director of Operational Manger
Bassett Historical Center
Bassett, Virginia

Waller Plantation Fieldale, Va
Courtesy of Pat Ross, Director of Operational Manger
Bassett Historical Center
Bassett, Virginia

Waller Plantation
Courtesy of Pat Ross, Director of Operational Manger
Bassett Historical Center
Bassett, Virginia

Dr. George & Sarah Waller
1880s
Courtesy of Pat Ross, Director of Operational Manger
Bassett Historical Center
Bassett, Virginia

Courtesy of Jon Willen, M.D.

Egyptian Building, Medical College of Virginia
Courtesy of Jodi L. Koste
Archivist Resources and Operations. VCU
(Associate Professor)
Tompkins-McCaw Library

Egyptian Building, Medical College of Virginia
Present Day
Courtesy of Jodi L. Koste
Archivist Resources and Operations. VCU
(Associate Professor)
Tompkins-McCaw Library

Dr. George E. Waller.
[Special to The Times-Dispatch.]
MARTINSVILLE, VA., February 2.—Dr. George E. Waller, one of the oldest and best known residents of Martinsville, died at his home on Broad Street at an early hour this morning, after an illness of two years. Dr. Waller was a surgeon in the Confederate army, and was a man of strong and interesting personality. He was for many years coroner of Henry County, and was also justice of the peace for a long period. Dr. Waller was a native of Henry County, and was seventy-six years old. He is survived by his wife, who was a Miss Putzell, and by four sons and two daughters. The sons are Will and George Waller, of Mississippi; Ed. P. Waller, of Schenectady, and Crawford Waller, of Chattanooga, Tenn. The daughters are Mrs. Mary Kuykendall and Mrs. George Clark, of Martinsville. The funeral will take place here to-morrow afternoon.

Courtesy of Pat Ross, Director of Operational Manger
Bassett Historical Center
Bassett, Virginia

The Author
P.D. Cotton

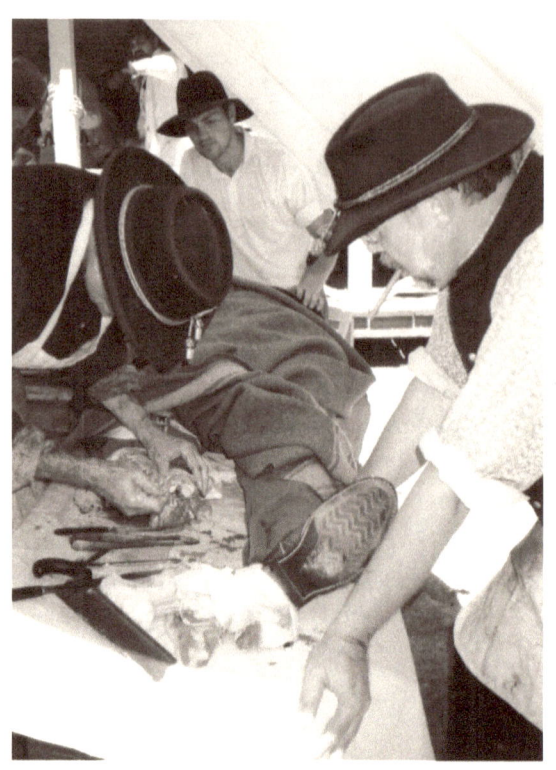

Confederate Staff
1998

Members of the 24th Virginia Hospital

Michael Jackson, David Cotton, Jon Willen, MD.
David Colley, Brian Lum and John Powell.

Lt Col. David Cotton, Major David Colley
Capitan John Powell, 1st. Sergeant Nathan Hays.

Officers Quarters at Fort Tejon Historical Park
Lebec, California.

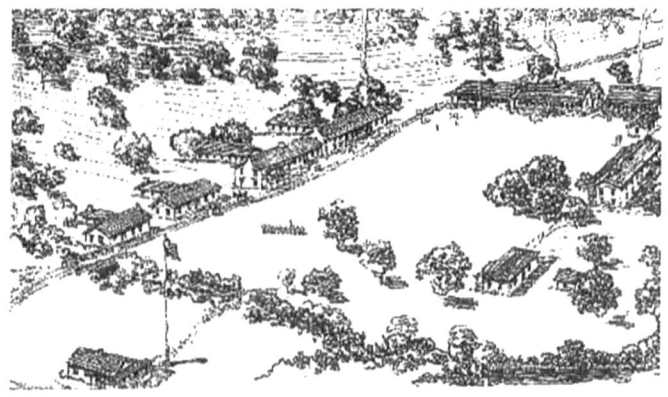

Fort Tejon, Ca
1850s

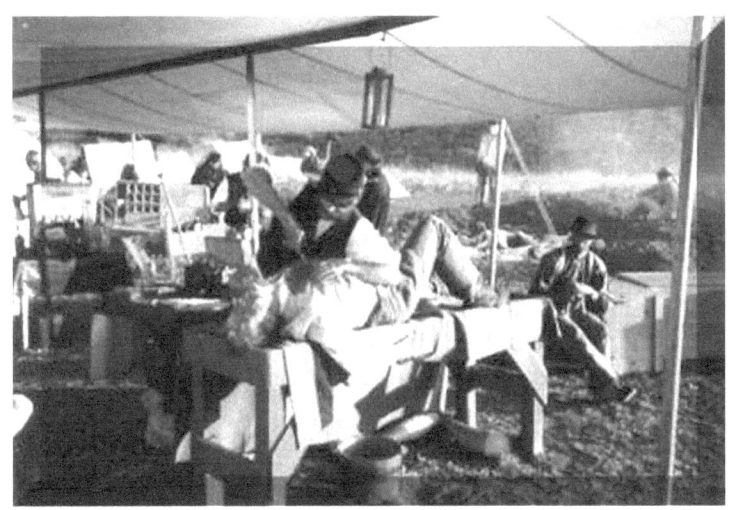

24th Virginia Field Hospital
Courtesy of the Author